FOR AND AGAINST FEMINISM

RELATED TITLES IN WOMEN'S STUDIES

Basis of the Bargain: Gender, Schooling & Jobs Carol O'Donnell

Caring for Australia's Children: Political & Industrial Issues in Child Care Deborah Brennan & Carol O'Donnell

Contemporary Feminist Thought Hester Eisenstein

Crossing Boundaries: Feminisms & the Critique of Knowledges Barbara Caine, E.A. Grosz & Marie de Lepervanche (eds)

Ethnicity, Class & Gender in Australia Gill Bottomley & Marie de Lepervanche (eds)

Female Crime: The Construction of Women in Criminology Ngaire Naffine

Feminist Challenges: Social & Political Theory Carole Pateman & Elizabeth Gross (eds)

Gender & Power R.W. Connell

Gender Agenda Terry Evans

Gender At Work Ann Game & Rosemary Pringle

Getting Equal: Labour Market Regulation and Women's Work Carol O'Donnell & Philippa Hall

Good & Mad Women: The Historical Construction of Femininity in Twentieth Century Australia Jill Julius Matthews

Program for Change Marian Sawer (ed.)

Subordination: Feminism & Social Theory Clare Burton

Teaching Gender? Sex Education & Sexual Stereotypes Tricia Szirom

Which Way Is Up? Essays on Class, Sex & Culture R.W. Connell

A Woman's Place: Women & Politics in Australia Marian Sawer & Marian Simms

Women, Social Science & Public Policy Jacqueline Goodnow & Carole Pateman (eds)

FOR AND AGAINST FEMINISM

A personal journey into feminist theory and history

ANN CURTHOYS

Allen & Unwin
Sydney Wellington London Boston

First published in 1988
Allen & Unwin Australia Pty Ltd
An Unwin Hyman company
8 Napier Street, North Sydney, NSW 2060 Australia

Allen & Unwin New Zealand Limited
60 Cambridge Terrace, Wellington, New Zealand

Unwin Hyman Limited
15–17 Broadwick Street, London W1V 1FP England

Allen & Unwin Inc.
8 Winchester Place, Winchester, Mass 01890 USA

National Library of Australia
Cataloguing-in-Publication entry:

Curthoys, Ann, 1945-
  For and against feminism.

  Includes index.
  ISBN 0 04 310021 X.

  1. Feminism. 2. Women's rights. 3. Women and
  socialism. I. Title

305.4'2

Library of Congress Catalog Card Number: 88–70248

Set in 10/11 Times by Times Graphics, Singapore
Printed by Kim Hup Lee, Singapore

Contents

Foreword
Meaghan Morris

In one of the essays in this book, Ann Curthoys describes the contributors to a feminist discussion of the family as 'lively and illuminating on the past, foggy on the present, and bewildered about the future'.

When I began reading *For and Against Feminism*, a flood of 'lively and illuminating' studies of the past was pouring from the presses and the TV screens for the Australian Bicentenary. Shortly after finishing the book, I had a befogging choice in the 1988 NSW State election between a Liberal Party promising state-wide to abolish Aboriginal Land Rights, and a Labor Party promising locally to fill in part of Port Hacking, and turn a beach now safe for children into a haven for deep-water yachts. Both parties made other 'promises' to interest groups here and there, but neither offered much anywhere to 'feminism'—except through 'health', 'housing' 'law and order', or 'education'. Collectively feminist sensibilities stirred only when Labor tried to discredit the Liberal leader by presenting his wife as 'pushy'. Then the anti-abortion, anti-homosexual Call to Australia Party quietly won half the balance of power in the Upper House—and announced support for Land Rights. Imagining a future from these mystifying shreds of my past and present, it's easy to feel, I must say, both foggy and bewildered.

One of the best things about reading Ann Curthoys' book now is that while it is a fascinating history of an Australian feminist experience, it is neither an attempt to return to the past, nor a rallying-call assuming that the problems of the present are simple, and future feminist directions obvious. Nor is *For and Against Feminism* a celebration of anxiety and confusion: from the first to the last essay in the book, Curthoys writes with the cheering lucidity of a thinker whose scepticism about all received wisdom (feminist wisdom included) is matched only by her confidence that difficult questions should—and can—be confronted.

At a time when sentimental left-wing recollections of the early 1970s are beginning to compete with myopic pragmatism and quack-remedy futurism as substitutes for new political thinking, Curthoys' 'personal journey' through feminism is as lively and illuminating about the present as it is critical of the past—and so is capable of imagining definite future possibilities.

The journey through theory and history represented by this book spans almost twenty years of feminist politics in Australia. Some readers will already be familiar with Ann Curthoys' essays, while for others *For and Against Feminism* will be a first encounter with debates that have lost none of their pertinence with the passing of time—or will make new and different sense when read in the changed circumstances of today. Still other readers may begin as I did, aware that Ann Curthoys' work had been 'important' to feminist historiography in Australia and to theories of women and work, yet having only the vaguest idea of what she had actually written.

One of the unfortunate side-effects of the otherwise vital activities of small journals in Australia is that writing which has fostered argument and research may remain inaccessible to a wider public, or even unknown to any but a small circle of initiates who happened to be around at the time. The journals are indispensable in providing arenas for experiment, for creating new spheres of debate, and in countering the deadly inertia of much academic and journalistic culture in Australia. But in the process, the substance of particular arguments may be marginalised to purely professional contexts. Then through hearsay, photocopy circuits and friendship networks, intellectual products may come to circulate only in the faded and intimidating form of personal *reputations*. As well as bringing a degree of repetitiveness to local debates, this tendency can encourage nostalgia in successive generations for 'the good old days' of their early activity—the details of which have become increasingly hazy. Meanwhile, the history of critical movements like feminism is sometimes still written and taught in Australia with reference primarily to British and American thinkers who could circulate their work, from the beginning, in solid paperback form.

Yet a collection such as *For and Against Feminism* offers much more than a compensation for, or a corrective to, present vagueness about the recent feminist past. The first essay in the book ('Women's Liberation and the writing of history', 1970) is legendary to feminist historians. However to read it for the first time today is not only better to understand retrospectively the emergence of feminist history in Australia, but to discover a new text that argues with exceptional clarity and pertinence *now* the case for women's history as a radical questioning of what writing history means, rather than as simply giving women a 'place' within the confines of an existing practice. This questioning is carried on and intensified by the rest of the book right through to its conclusion—in which 'feminism', as well as 'history', is now open to the kind of redefinition that suggests beginnings rather than endings.

Reading Ann Curthoys' essays today, a startling consistency emerges to give shape to the collection. It isn't the consistency of a partisan who has been saying the same thing for twenty years, and still less the consistency of an ideologue of correct lines in politics or theory. Curthoys documents and discusses fundamental changes in her own thinking about the family, housework, childcare, and the sexual division of labour, as well as broad shifts in the relations between feminism and other political movements, and between conflicting versions of feminism. Ann Curthoys' consistency is rather in the operation of her persistently irreverent and relentless critical spirit. She takes nothing for granted, leaves no cliché or piety unexamined: even the bottom-line vocabulary of modern feminism—'sexism', 'patriarchy', 'the women's movement', 'feminism' itself—is questioned for the failures and compromises it has entailed, as well as for its positive uses.

There are no 'good old days' of feminism for this book, and it isn't in any sense a simple retrospective. Because the essays are framed by a story of how they came to be written, as well as a commentary on how the author now understands the contexts in which she was working, there is in *For and Against Feminism* an exciting sense of exchange between past and present, experience and analysis, adventure and criticism. At the same time, there is no rosy glow of innocence emanating even from what Curthoys calls the 'heady' days of women's liberation. What seems remarkable (at least to this reader) is how sharp her criticisms were of the problems then already emerging from feminist attempts to generalise about 'women', and how prophetic some of her warnings about the consequences have been. She has always contested and resisted the gentrification of feminist politics: refusing to ignore or marginalise questions of class and race oppression, mistrustful of too great a dependence by feminists on an interventionist State, much of Ann Curthoys' work may well turn out to have an immediacy and a usefulness more obvious to more feminists in the 1990s than at the times when it was written.

Somewhere in the book, Curthoys notes that the experience of preparing it made her realise how autobiographical intellectual work really is. Reading that made me realise why I had so much enjoyed the book as a *narrative*—to the point of skipping to the end at one stage to see how the story turned out. Apart from its interest as a participant's history of modern feminist thought in Australia, *For and Against Feminism* has such a strong narrative charge because of the movement in so many of the essays between acts of theorisation, moments of reflection, and the experience of everyday living. Some movement like this is perhaps what was assumed or promised by the old saying 'the personal is political'. It's a saying that is all the more appropriate to this book because it *isn't* a series of intimate revelations and confessions, but an intellectual journey —one that advances by making explicit connections between the author's changing social experience and her theoretical work.

What is not quite appropriate to *For and Against Feminism* is the reverse proposition: 'the political is (only) personal'. Rather than deriving all political problems supposedly significant to 'women' from her own immediate environment, Ann Curthoys has stressed in all her work the necessity to come to terms with and to learn from the experience of other women—for many of whom the constraints and dilemmas of gender may usually take second place to those of race and class. She has also always argued that feminism can ill afford to dismiss or devalue the social oppressions and struggles confronted by vast numbers of men. The political is 'personal' in *For and Against Feminism* only in the sense that Curthoys' work insists on a rigorous rethinking of the 'personal' to open it up to the possibility of recognising difference in other women and men— rather than enfolding the notion in the narcissistic reveries of a middle-class feminist 'lifestyle'.

It is perhaps Ann Curthoys' capacity to develop and change her own work by engaging with the experience of others that makes *For and Against Feminism* such a fascinating autobiography. In that sense, her own book is the beginning of an answer to one of the bewildering questions that, after considering her past and present, she poses in the end about the possible future of feminism—'how to regain a belief in the possibility and effectiveness of collective action across gender and racial boundaries without losing that understanding of specific cultural situations that we have painfully begun to acquire'.

Acknowledgements

Most of the chapters in this book have appeared in print before. I am grateful to the publishers listed below for permission to reprint:
'Women's Liberation and the writing of history' originally appeared as 'Historiography and Women's Liberation' in *Arena* 22, 1970. 'Politics and Sisterhood' appeared in *Arena* 62, 1983. 'Housework' appeared in the first issue of *Mejane* in 1971. 'Men and childcare' originally appeared as 'Men and Childcare in the Feminist Utopia' in *Refractory Girl* no. 10, 1976. 'Women—a "Reserve Army of Labour"?' appeared in *Refractory Girl* 13, 1977–78. 'Explaining the Sexual Division of Labour' appeared first in *Refractory Girl* 18–19, 1979–80, and in a revised version in Norma Grieve and Patricia Grimshaw (eds) *Australian Women: Feminist Perspectives* Melbourne: Oxford University Press, 1981. 'Colonial women's history' appeared as 'History in a Vacuum' in *Hecate* X,1, 1984. 'The Family and Feminism' appeared in *Hecate* XI,1, 1985. 'Radical Feminism' first appeared as an untitled essay in Robyn Rowland (ed.), *Women Who Do and Women Who Don't Join the Women's Movement* London: Routledge & Kegan Paul, 1983. 'Women and Class' has previously been published in slightly different versions: in Anna Rutherford and Kirsten Holst Petersen (eds) *A Double Colonization: Women and Colonial Writing* Aarhus: Dangaroo Press, 1986, and in Carole Ferrier (ed.) *Angry Women* Sydney: Hale & Iremonger, 1987. The version that appears here includes several paragraphs from another article, 'Feminism and the Classes' *Arena* 64, 1983. 'A short history of feminism, 1970–1984' was originally published under the title 'The Women's Movement and Social Justice', in Dorothy Broom (ed.) *Unfinished Business: Women and Social Justice* Sydney: Allen & Unwin, 1984. The version published here is a little longer. 'The emergence of a feminist labour history' originally appeared under the title 'Towards a Feminist Labour History' in Ann Curthoys, Susan Eade and Peter Spearritt (eds) *Women at Work* Canberra: Australian Society for the Study of Labour History, 1975. 'The Sexual Division of Labour: Theoretical Arguments' appeared in Norma Grieve and Ailsa Burns (eds) *Australian Women: New Feminist Perspectives* Melbourne: Oxford University Press, 1986.

Preface

I wrote this book for several reasons. Most of the essays I've written about women and the women's movement are in small Australian journals or hard-to-find books. In bringing the essays together in this way, I hope to make the debates I've been involved in available to a wider audience than hitherto. There is, as well, unpublished material in this collection which it seemed to me would make more sense set alongside the already printed work than published alone. Further, I found that I had reached a point in my work where I needed to take stock, to look back over and reflect upon the road I'd travelled before I could go on to new endeavours. I hope the book works not merely as a personal reassessment, but also assists in a more general process of working out future directions for feminist theory, history, and politics.

This book, then, has several purposes and can be read in several ways. It is in part a history of the ideas and debates of modern feminism, especially as they were worked out in Australia from 1970 onwards. To read it as such you would probably read it straight through, from beginning to end. If you were interested, however, primarily in the problem of the relationship between marxism and feminism—two world views, often seen to be in conflict but also very much in dialogue—then you would consult mainly Parts III and IV. But if you've picked the book up mainly to find out about feminist theory on women and work then I suggest you concentrate on chapters 8 and 9, 13, and the whole of Part V. If you want to extend this to an interest in the history of women and work you could also take in chapters 6 and 19. For those interested in Australian women's history generally, try chapters 3, 5, and 18 as well.

The introduction to each chapter establishes when and why it was written. Where the essay has been previously published, I have made this clear, and publication details can be found in the acknowledgements at the beginning of the book. I have generally resisted the temptation to edit out sections I no longer agree with, as this is meant to be a history as well as a work of contemporary theory and argument. I have, however, in the case of some of the more recent essays added some additional material, where I felt the argument was cryptic, or hard to follow. Wherever I've done this,

I've informed the reader in the introduction. In the process of editing, some essays have been shortened while others have had material, edited out by the original publisher, restored.

I am grateful to all those who have helped provide a congenial political and intellectual environment within which to think, act, and write. I thank first those who participated in the Women's Liberation movement in the early 1970s in Sydney, who helped me sort out my own thinking, especially Camille Guy, Lesley Lynch, Mary Murnane, Lyndall Ryan, and Anne Summers. Those I encountered later who provided important intellectual stimulus include Kay Daniels, Ann Game, Carol Johnston, Marilyn Lake, Jan Larbalestier, Susan Magarey, Jeannie Martin, Margaret Power, Rosemary Pringle, and Kathy Robinson. A particular thanks to Lyndall Ryan for allowing a paper we wrote jointly so long ago to be reprinted here.

There are several men whom I wish to thank as well: especially my husband John Docker for his constant support and helpful advice; Jack Barbalet, John Bern, Peter Bryant, and Bob Connell for valuable commentary; Peter Spearritt for being an energetic and congenial co-editor on the *Women at Work* collection in 1975; and my colleague Gunther Kress, who suggested at just the right moment that I put this collection together.

I wrote several chapters while a research fellow at the Social Justice Project at the Australian National University in 1985, and thank Pat Troy, the convenor of that project, for his support.

PART I

Women's liberation: beginnings

1

Women's liberation and the writing of history

I joined the women's liberation group in Glebe, Sydney, in January 1970. You didn't actually 'join', you just went along. During that year I attended discussion meetings regularly, where I imbibed and helped hammer out the basic principles of women's liberation. I was working on a PhD thesis in Australian history at the time women's liberation started up and I began to think about the implications of women's liberation for my historical work.

During 1970 we in the Glebe group of women's liberation had been reading a lot of American women's liberation material, often in journal or newspaper form, or roneoed reprints. Books which are now regarded as key texts, such as Juliet Mitchell's Woman's Estate (1970), Shulamith Firestone's The Dialectic of Sex (1970) and Germaine Greer's The Female Eunuch (1970) all appeared on Australian bookshop shelves somewhat after we had done our initial journey of theoretical discovery. It was the first chapter of Kate Millett's Sexual Politics (1970), which we read in roneoed form, together with American journals such as Off Our Backs, which were the most influential. At the same time, Julie Riggs's book on Australian women, In Her Own Right (1969), came to my attention, and it included a chapter on Australian women's history by the Left labour historian, Ian Turner. The chapter gave me the opening I needed to write an article about the implications of women's liberation ideas for the writing of Australian history. There was no women's liberation journal or newspaper at this time, and I sent the article to the Melbourne marxist journal, Arena. 'Historiography and Women's Liberation' was a kind of manifesto, and attracted considerable attention for several years, until its purpose was superseded from about 1975 by the appearance of feminist works on Australian history.

1970

The 'woman question' has rarely been considered as fundamental to a critique of capitalist society either by the Left or by the women's movements themselves. The Left has too often seen women's claims as admissable, but peripheral to the real task of analysing what capitalist society *is* and why a different kind of society must be established. Women's movements of the older middle-class feminist type have seen their task as establishing equality with men within existing society, their vital concern for equality preventing them from arriving at any sort of attack on the existing capitalist society as a whole. As long as this disjunction between radical and feminist critiques and demands continues, neither the liberation of women nor of mankind generally will be possible.

The idea of women's liberation is fundamental to a critique of capitalist society, because what is at issue is not simply the position of women, but the whole question of sex-role differentiation. This, of course, has occurred in all societies; nevertheless it is realistic to make a specific analysis of the function of sex-role differentiation in our specific, capitalist society. Role division according to sex is at the basis of the present family structure and the rigidity of the work situation—it involves a sharp separation between public and private life, between work and politics on the one hand and home and family on the other. Men are expected to be responsible workers in a labour force run along authoritarian lines, to be participants in public and political life, dominant, aggressive and confident in style. They are expected at once to support financially and ideologically control their women while using them as emotional anchors in the home, the refuge from the competitive and harassing world of work. Women are expected to be primarily responsible in the home for housework and children, and to be passive in public life. They are to accept less pay and a highly marginal status when they do work outside the home, and to be generally irresponsible, irrational, passive and trivial. These stereotypes clearly harm and distort both sexes.

The socialisation of production brought about by the industrial revolution has not included the home, housework and childcare. In fact, the effect has been, by the creation of labour-saving domestic tools, to *further* isolate housework. The family functions as the stabiliser, the consumption unit and the isolator in capitalist society. Men and women are thus divided in the workforce itself, because of the marginal and threatening status of women in industry; they are divided in their relation to children—and in the possible behaviour available to each sex.

Yet while the critique concerning social division according to sex is a general one and not limited to the concept of women's liberation, there is a real reason why much of the critique has come from and will continue to come from women's liberation movements. This is because women are in an especially contradictory situation under capitalism—they are allowed educational and other opportunities to participate in public life and the public economy, but are still regarded as the essential guardians of children, and are still the prisoners of family and social limitation. Women have therefore been able to formulate specific demands, capable of attacking these sex-differentiated structures. Here the analogy with the black movement is relevant—just as the breakdown of racism in society is bound up with the development of black movements and selfconsciousness, so the breakdown of rigid sex-role differentiation is bound up with the fortunes of women's movements.

Most of the above analysis is implicit in Anna Yeatman's 'The Liberation of Women', in *Arena* 21. She rightly calls for analyses to be made by women's liberation movements to enable them to proceed, and one of the essential parts of this analysis is a 'new historiography, detailed studies of the place and functions of women and the family through history'. That this *is* essential is shown by the fact that the continued reliance of much of the women's liberation movement on the analyses of Engels, derived from Morgan, is severely limiting its understanding of why the present situation exists.[1] However, we should not only seek to explain why the family exists, but also attempt a much more far reaching study of why sex differentiation in all its aspects has occurred, how it has affected the lives of both men and women and how it is related to the maintenance of, or change in, entrenched social and power structures. Yet there is reason, too, to emphasise the effects of the division on *women*, for it is women who have been left out of history, because of that discipline's preoccupation with public life and politics, and because it is women, who, for the reasons given, will probably be most involved in the movement for change in sex roles, and who therefore need to be armed with historical perspectives and explanations.

A 'history of women', then, should do more than restore women to the pages of history books. It must analyse why public life has been considered to be the focus of history, and why public life has been so thoroughly occupied by men. We must find out how the assumptions of female inferiority in public life and subordination in the home have operated in history, and ask why some societies differentiate more than others. We must especially find out the effect of industrialisation and Christianity on the position of women. The concepts usually operating in historiography, defining what is important, must be questioned.

In Australia it is difficult to know where to start: these problems have never been considered seriously. For most, a consideration of women in history would appear trivial. Moreover, historians themselves are still bound within the rigidly defined sex roles of this society: male historians see 'women's matters' as trivial and not the stuff of history. They tend to see the behaviour of women as biologically rather than largely, if not wholly, socially determined and so see no reason to understand or analyse that behaviour. Female historians have been affected by a desire to succeed as *people*, to submerge their feminine identity and by an abhorrence of the feminist stereotype. Just as the few women who are successful in trade unions and political parties tend to be those who have played down their social position as women and have set out to prove their personal ability and worth, so academic women tend to avoid studying or talking about women in society. The growth and impact of women's liberation movements will make it easier for female historians to attain the confidence necessary to consider women in history and social divisions according to sex, and will probably stimulate male historians to take these issues seriously.

Women do not appear in most Australian histories in any important way. The nature and effect of the family in Australian society is not discussed. Sexual habits and beliefs have not been studied, nor have the rate and reasons for the entry of women into the workforce. When women do enter history, it is either to discuss the beginnings of women's entry into political and public life,[2] to see women's behaviour as a demonstration of the loosening of British formality in the colonies, to see women as the builders of early colonial social elites, or to present a picture of the hard-working bush mum. Until the 1860s they were mainly what we need more of, the symbols of a stable settled society, and the holders of very necessary domestic skills. They were the bearers of children, the future hopes of the colonial society. Yet while questions of female immigration may be discussed in detail, the importance of the sex-role division is not seen; *why* women so much represented stability.[3]

The most recent historical work in the field of women in history is Ian Turner's chapter 'Prisoners in Petticoats: a shocking history of female emancipation in Australia', in Julie Rigg's *In Her Own Right* (Nelson, 1969). The problems involved in carrying out Anna Yeatman's plea for a new historiography of women, particularly in writing Australian history, can be discussed in relation to Turner's work. His chapter is not meant to be the result of detailed research or particularly scholarly analysis, but is rather an attempt to draw together what is already known into a suggestive, impressionistic overview of the subject.

Turner has discussed the history of women in Australia from

1788 to 1945 in terms of how they lived, and in describing the haphazard, rather stunted development of feminist movements. He begins with convict society, where women were doubly exploited— 'first in their labour and then in their sex'. Convict women were frequently compelled to serve their masters sexually, and the wives of officers had neither property nor independent employment, but rather a life of petty social rounds and domestic responsibilities. The pioneering and pastoral industry required female help, if possible, in clearing and establishing the station, managing the domestic side of the establishment and providing and caring for children. As squatters became more secure, women provided stability and continuity in pastoral society. Among poorer farmers the pattern was similar except that women worked harder both on the farm and in the home. In urban society working-class women worked at poor jobs for little pay, and then escaped into marriage, where they kept the home and brought up the children. Middle-class women did not marry to escape work, as no work was available to them, but they too were primarily responsible for home and family. The difference lay in the availability of domestic help. Whereas the working-class mother was forced to work extremely hard because of primitive tools, the middle-class mother frequently did not have enough to do, and spent much of her time in leisurely pursuits, charity organisations and temperance movements. A significant difference between city and country was that city women had greater opportunities for sexual, educational and even occupational movement.

Turner says this basic division of labour according to sex continued right up to the Second World War. The First World War had little impact on female employment patterns in Australia, as it had in England. The nineteenth-century pattern continued throughout the Depression and up to World War Two. But in WW II there was total mobilisation of labour. Women were employed in the armed forces and in new industries; creches developed and domestic service disappeared. This pattern has been further established and developed in the years since.

Having described the situation of women in general, Turner develops his second strand—a discussion of women's movements. These, he points out, were almost entirely middle-class; working-class women, for reasons he does not go into, never objected strongly to their inferior and unstable status in industry, nor to being housewives and mothers within the confines of their own homes. Nor does he explain *why* middle-class women in the late nineteenth and early twentieth century sought educational and employment opportunities, hitherto denied them. He suggests that the vote was never an issue for Australian women, as they were 'handed the vote on a plate'. Feminists sought to act independently in 'raising the moral condition of the land', which can otherwise be seen as an attack on the double standard in sexual and other behavioural morality. Hence the proximity of temperance, wowserish movements and women's movements, a connection which still persists in some women's organisations. The moralism was symbolic of the degree to which earlier women's movements were so middle-class, so unable to question (fundamentally) assumptions about the primary responsibility of women in the family. They argued that women should be able to choose a career as an alternative to the home if they so wished, and moreover that it *was* possible to play the role of housewife and mother, and have a career as well. To extend the analysis into the present, I would add that the radicalism of women's liberation, still a middle-class movement but of a rather different kind, lies in its rejection of this approach. Women's liberation now argues that having children involves equal and similar responsibilities for men and women, that housework is not inherently women's work, and that radical social reorganisation is required before women will be really able to pursue their intellectual, occupational, artistic or social interests to the full. Ian Turner is wrong when he says that the preconditions for equality had been established by 1945. They have not been established yet.

The chapter seems to me an original attempt to see generally the role in society of women in Australia. But while it is interesting in its creation of a picture of what it may have been like to be a woman in this country, it fails to grasp the very profound relationship between the social roles expected of women, the kind of economy being set up in Australia, and the development of liberal-democratic political traditions. He fails to stress the importance of the family as a fundamental unit of social organisation, cutting across but nevertheless very much affected by class. The individual family concept, because it does cut across class lines and because it is so important to the quality of individual lives and to the social structure and the economy as a whole, helped weld the society together through a common set of attitudes.

Again, Turner does not show that Australian ideologies have been heavily male-oriented, as the 'mateship' ideology on the one hand and the liberal and Christian ideal of the family on the other, indicate.

All this stems from his concept of a history of women: because he isolates the question of 'the position of women', he tends to describe the changes in the female situation without explaining them and doesn't see how the female situation he described had ramifications for the whole of Australian history.

Both Anna Yeatman and Ian Turner point to the tremendous gaps in Australian historiography and in our understanding of the cultural traditions, social attitudes and organisational structures which have set up such divisions between men and women. The analyses they stimulate have scarcely begun, but as we proceed, we should be careful that we do not confine our analyses to 'the position of women' but are able to integrate analyses concerning women with the mainstream of historical inquiry.

2

The theory of women's liberation

In January 1971 the women's liberation groups in Sydney held a conference. There were many papers given, distributed first in roneoed form, and a lot of lively discussion. Lyndall Ryan and I wrote a joint paper, somewhat mysteriously entitled 'Up from Radicalism: Problems of Organisation in Sydney Women's Liberation'. We were at this time both postgraduate students in history, and had both been active in left-wing politics, in particular the movement opposing Australian involvement in the Vietnam War.

The first section of our paper, printed here, dealt with the overall analysis that we thought women's liberation provided. It is interesting now to see not only what we did say but also to note which words and concepts we didn't, notably 'sexism' and 'patriarchy', to name two which became common currency later.

1971

The way in which we think the position of women, and therefore the relationship between men and women in society, will change, depends on the way we think society is structured in the first place. In our analysis of the structure of society we do not see all power as concentrated in the hands of the state, or of a few monopolies, but rather as lying in the sum total of the cultural, social, economic, and political traditions of that society. While powerful institutions such as the state rely ultimately on force, they do not often do so in any immediate sense because they can rely on a wide acceptance of the legitimacy of their power. The perpetuation of some of the most powerful institutions affecting women as women, such as marriage and the family, relies partly on state sanction but most profoundly on widespread cultural and social acceptance.

It is through a total cultural analysis of society, rather than a conspiratorial one, that the situation of women becomes comprehensible. And this analysis is not restricted to capitalist society, but extends to the totality of Western European culture of which our society is a part. We are concerned here with every male-dominated society, whether it be capitalist, communist, or socialist. Apart from the obvious social, economic, and political oppression of women in capitalist societies there is a much deeper, more insidious cultural oppression based on all the myths and legends that have been created about women. How, for example, do we combat the assumptions about women, whether they be in the novels of Tolstoy, Patrick White, Norman Mailer, the music of the Rolling Stones, the operas of Glinka, Wagner, and Verdi, the films of Peckinpah, Eisenstein, Tony Richardson, or Godard, or the advertising media, or even the revolutionary program for women in the Cuban revolution? It is in our cultural mores that the assumptions about women are so deeply entrenched, perpetuated, and practised in their crudest forms. It is here that the oppression of women goes beyond the traditional class barriers. And it is here that we have to start to smash these myths, for unless we can change the whole cultural orientation of women, no revolution is going to bring us the liberation we are seeking.

And yet it is true that there are structural aspects of society which, while undermined by changing social attitudes, nevertheless persist. The breakdown of existing attitudes held by and about women will be impeded by the structural difficulty in choosing alternative lifestyles. For example, whatever a woman's self-concept, how can she now really pursue her own interests satisfactorily if she has children; or alternatively how can she spend the time she wishes to spend with her children if she is financially forced to work? Again, a woman, however much she ignores social pressures, still cannot do whatever work she wishes. A woman who does not wish to have children can still be forced to do so. Yet another example of the way large social structures oppress the individual woman, whatever her attitudes, is the structure of the workforce and especially the notion of a family wage. As long as the work structure is the way it is, where men have to work at least 40 hours a week, and continuously from year to year to get enough money and the sort of satisfaction which arises from gaining some responsibility in their working life, then it is virtually impossible for couples to share the care of children with any ease. That is, as long as men cannot be freed from the continuity and long hours of work while they are fathers of young children, women on a large scale will find it hard to be free. Closely linked with this is the problem of the availability of childcare centres, the creation of which will not only require a change in consciousness but also community activities and public campaigns.

Thus cultural traditions, social attitudes, and powerful social structures are mutually supportive and interdependent. This implies that the strategy of women's liberation must be to attack all three. We do not concentrate only on engaging women in an attempt to change the state by election or political revolution. Nor are we only a social and personal movement which is essentially apolitical. Rather we see women's liberation as a movement which is working for social and individual change, and which sees that at certain points in this process, campaigns of a highly political nature are necessary.

To put it another way, we see women's liberation as working for revolution, but not the sort of revolution which is an event that takes two or three days, in which there is shooting and hanging. 'It will be a long, drawn out process in which new people will be created, capable of renovating society so that the revolution will not replace one elite with another, but rather will create a new anti-authoritarian society, with new anti-authoritarian people who in their turn will reorganise the society so that it will become a non-alienated human society, free from war, hunger, and exploitation.' These words of Rudi Dutschke are about the closest we have heard to the ideal some of us are seeking. Susan Sontag has stated the problem even more bluntly. For her revolution means 'not only creating political and economic justice but releasing and validating personal, as well as social, energies of all kinds, including erotic ones'.

When women's liberation first emerged in Sydney, our sternest critics were the leaders of the Left. To them we were a group whose personal concerns had broken class lines. We had split the Left. To us, however, it was quite apparent that the Left had never considered women in a revolutionary perspective, expecting us to remain its faithful servants and supporters in the great struggle. We therefore had two alternatives: work within the various existing Left groups attempting to convince them of our validity, or go our own way and create our own movement. We had no choice but to pursue the latter.

We had not worked out our own problems, we wished to work at our own pace, and we had to escape the standover tactics of our so-called sympathetic supporters among the males. Above all we found that the authoritarian structure of left-wing politics was inimical to women's liberation.

One of the most serious problems in left-wing politics is that by their highly organised nature, in their total absorption of people's time, in their mechanical and frustrating procedures, the people involved in them become increasingly removed from the impulses which led to their joining, and isolated from the society which initially inspired them into left-wing action. Many feel that the atmosphere among leftwingers who develop intense hatreds of one another is destructive, that few real friendships develop and that even the strongest are liable to be broken by a political divergence. In other words, in the name of working for a desirable end, Leftists employ as their *means* social relationships and manipulative styles which we see as having no part of their ideal society. If a revolution is not a quick seizure of power but a long social revolution with a political aspect, however, then the means *are* the ends. Immediate behaviour constitutes the revolution itself. For women's liberation this means that the daily attack on sex roles is one of the most fundamental ways in which the liberation of women will occur.

It is clear looking back over the past year that a lot has been discussed, involving a considerable number of people, in what has been quite an original way. We have also had contact with new people and with a new, if rather loose, body of ideas. One effect has been to make us rethink our whole self-concept and consequently our relationships with other people. In different ways the ideas of women's liberation have influenced our work and our intellectual interests more than we originally envisaged.

3

Housework

The influence of women's liberation on our intellectual pursuits was indeed very considerable. Soon after the January conference, in February 1971, a group of women began producing Sydney's (and, I think, Australia's) first women's liberation newspaper, Mejane. *The first issue illustrates the range of issues we thought important: work, reproductive control, women in politics, education, and women's history. It included an article on discrimination against married women working in Broken Hill, news on abortion campaigns, a story on Louisa Lawson and* The Dawn, *an account of childcare provision, another on International Women's Day, an interview with Wendy Bacon (anti-censorship activist and recently briefly imprisoned) on the lives of women in prison, discussion of sexism in schools and of a conference on women and the movement against the Vietnam War, a review of* The Female Eunuch, *a report on the New South Wales Women's Liberation conference of January 1971, and reports on various group activities.*

From the beginning of women's liberation, the question of women's work was regarded as crucial. In the first few issues of Mejane *we printed interviews with women about their work. We began with housewives, and I wrote the introduction to the transcribed and edited interviews. I signed it merely 'Ann', it being common practice in* Mejane *and other women's liberation contexts to use first names only. Sometimes, though, we used surnames as well. The other members of the collective, I find now from the back page of the first issue, were: Gale Kelly (then an artist, who has since died); Sue Bellamy (then a postgraduate history student, now a potter), Louise, Heather, Camille (then a journalist, now returned to New Zealand and a television columnist for the New Zealand* Listener*), Lesley Gray (then a teacher, now a senior public servant in the New South Wales Ministry of Education), Beverley (then and now an architect),*

Barbara Levy, Kate (Kate Jennings, then still a student, now a writer living in the US), Liz Hanna, Lyndall (now Reader in women's studies at Flinders University in South Australia), Robynne Murphy, Julie Gibson, Mavis Robertson, and Joyce Stevens (then as now a Communist Party activist).

I don't think any of these women were full-time mothers and housewives, though some of them had been. At this time in my life I knew very few, if any, people in the social situation I was analysing.

1971

When thinking about the situation of women in our society I am again and again brought back to the realisation that in trying to grasp the precise nature of the oppression of women I keep a stereotype called 'housewife' in my head which helps to summon up all sorts of images of unpaid unrecognised work, drudgery, petty repetitive tasks, powerlessness, unfulfilment, watching patronising housewives' television programs, Roselands, Dita Cobb, Beauty and the Beast, the unspeakably rude and patronising John Laws, tiny demanding children screaming all day and destroying all hope of privacy or sustained thought or creative activity. It is a picture of life from which I and others in women's liberation recoil, and hope desperately but not terribly confidently to escape.

Of course the oppression of women goes much further than the fact that housewives but never househusbands exist. It reaches into the total cultural, economic, political, sexual, and social life of women. Yet, because being a housewife is something that only women do, and because of its nature as a peculiarly dependent occupation, thinking seriously and in detail about the situation of the housewife does help us to understand the situation of women in general. For of course we are all at least part-time housewives.

We should try and evaluate housewifery as a possibility for women. In the light of our understanding of how women are affected by the housewife role, we must also consider all sorts of alternatives—for us as women, and for humanity to cope with housekeeping and childrearing.

In an attempt to learn more about the reality of being a house-wife in Australian society today, *Mejane* interviewed two Sydney housewives to learn their ideas about their daily existence. These interviews stand for themselves. Yet I would like to add that I think that both interviews indicate how complex the choice between 'home' and 'work' is for both working-class and middle-class women.

For working-class women, work offers much-needed and in many cases essential finance. It also represents to some an escape from the isolation and boredom of the home, an opportunity to meet people. Because of most women's general lack of skilled training and the widespread job discrimination against them, however, the jobs available to most women are generally low-paid and monotonous, carried out under appalling material and psychological conditions. So, if the financial need is anything less than essential, many women prefer being a housewife and bringing up their children. While being a housewife may entail hard work, inadequate labour-saving devices, difficult budgeting on the husband's low wage, boredom and isolation, it also represents for many women the pleasures of close contact with young children, a certain amount of personal freedom in choosing when to do what, and some time at least for relaxation and recreation.

For the middle-class woman the choice is a little different. The financial push to go to work is not pressing, but since she may often have a real alternative in the sense of an at least partially interesting job, she feels acutely the characteristic boredom, frustration, and isolation of being a housewife. She may have time for social-work activities or personal hobbies, but may feel dilettantish and wish to develop her talents or interests in a more systematic and socially central way.

The choice facing women is thus a difficult one. The nature and meaning of this choice has been one of the central concerns of Sydney Women's Liberation during the last year. Those of us in Women's Lib. who jumped in early, employing the housewife stereotype in such a way as to suggest that women should go out to work rather than be housewives, quickly learned that outside work as it now exists is not a real alternative for many women.

The recent Women's Liberation January conference discussed this in some detail. Seeing that the immediate choice is ultimately not a real choice at all, we spent some time trying to work out various alternatives to the existing patterns. These alternatives, we felt, were necessarily long-range idealistic ones, involving a considerable change in the structure of society as a whole.

Two papers were given trying to define alternatives. One, by Virginia, advocating the abolition of the nuclear family, led to a lively discussion. Most agreed with her that the family was a very poor institution in the way it isolated its members, gave children limited experience of other children and adults, kept women isolated from wider experiences, and was the basis of many neurotic relationships. But several women wished to go further, and say that within the family women were parasitic as housewives and incompetent as mothers. Others felt this view distrusted individuals and preferred state solutions such as childcare centres. Some women argued also that the nuclear family as it existed did provide emotional sustenance of an intimate kind rarely found elsewhere in society. Mothers did form close relationships with their children. Any alternative would have to be able also to provide close personal relationships.

We went on to consider various alternatives in detail: communes, extended families, childcare centres, preschool education. There was a long debate on communes—how realistic now, how viable, the pitfalls, the problem of privacy. The instance of a serious project for communal living in Canberra was discussed. We also talked about childcare centres at some length. Some feared the effect of extending the present authoritarian education system even further back into a child's life, but most agreed that, as an ideal, preschool centres—readily available 24 hours a day—would benefit both mother and child. I think we did not approach sufficiently the crucially related issue of how fathers and children could obtain better relationships, to the point where the roles of mother and father do not differ.

A paper by Joyce on the economy was discussed at length. We considered short-term and long-term economic changes necessary if real alternative methods of doing the housewife's job are to be established. Changes discussed by Joyce included equal pay, end of employment discrimination, maternity and paternity leave with full pay. Yet these measures, while making it easier for women to enter the workforce for more reward than at present, do not confront the twin issues of how housework is to be done and children cared for.

We discussed the idea of pay for housewives, a suggestion which has been both supported and opposed by people in women's liberation. The arguments for include: it allows a woman to be financially independent; it raises the status of the occupation; if the job were paid men might be more easily inclined to do it, and so it would lose its present rigid sex role. The arguments against were various. Pay for housewives would mean that women with low-paid jobs would prefer to stay at home while women with higher-paid more interesting jobs would work and send their children to a day-nursery. So those women who most needed human contact and stimulation would be the very people who would stay at home. Another difficulty would be the problem of how to establish a rate of payment within the present wages structure. Further, if housework is isolating and boring the real problem is not monetary but psychological and social. There is a need to find ways of doing the same things in more interesting, efficient and possibly communal ways.

The point reached in many women's liberation discussions is one where there is a recognition of the complexity of the problem. We fear a solution which extends mass capitalist methods even further than now—into the home and life of a very young child. But we also oppose the present situation where 'work' is authoritarian and demanding and the home isolated, where women live in a highly individual—essentially feudal—position within a competitive capitalist society.

We oppose both the feudal and the capitalist solutions to people's personal problems, and their definition of women. But so-called socialist solutions which do not recognise the needs for privacy, individuality, choice, and freedom will not be our solution either.

PART II

*Women's liberation:
heady days*

4

Men and childcare

After travelling with my husband through Asia and living in London between May 1973 and June 1974, I returned to Australia and gave birth to a son in November 1974. Now living in Canberra, John and I shared the work of looking after our son, and I worked part-time as a research assistant on a project compiling an annotated guide to records concerning women in Australia.

The experience of mothering led me to think more about the implications of sexual differences in childcaring for social organisation generally. I wrote the following paper, the first I'd written on women's liberation issues since Mejane *in 1971, for a Feminism and Anarchism conference in Canberra in October 1975. The first paragraph indicates a disillusionment to some extent with the movement which I had found so exciting only a few years earlier. And it is interesting to note that the term 'women's liberation' had already disappeared, to be replaced by the blander 'women's movement', and the older 'feminism', the latter a term we'd avoided earlier for its 'bourgeois' connotations. And I note that the term 'patriarchal' appears in my own work, for the first time. I sent 'Men and Childcare in the Feminist Utopia' to the* Refractory Girl *collective in Sydney, who published it. It attracted a lot of attention at the time. Several interviews on ABC radio, in particular, resulted.*

1975

Many feminists are in the process of defining their dissatisfaction with the women's movement as it is in Australia today. There is dissatisfaction with many of the women's centres and services set up by the movement, dissatisfaction with the level of feminist theory we are developing, dissatisfaction that as the women's movement grows in size it is diluting its perspectives, programs, and aims. These dissatisfactions can be summed up as a loss of direction which itself is a losing sight of our ends, our ultimate goals. We have not, that is to say, a clear notion of our feminist utopia. This paper is an attempt to redefine that utopia. In the process it argues that unless we reappraise our notion of how men fit into that utopia the women's movement will become increasingly limited, powerless, co-opted, and middle-class, and will finally subside as it has done in the past.

The feminist utopia as I see it is a non-sexist society, but more than that, a society where other structural inequalities and oppressions are eliminated, whether based on class, race, age, or whatever. The older term 'women's liberation' expresses this dual aim better than do our 'new' terms 'feminist' and 'the women's movement', but probably we are stuck with 'feminist' as a shorter and more linguistically flexible term. In my ideal society there are no distinctions between men and women, though certain differences will remain—women will give birth, and there are differences in sexuality itself. The ending of sex roles will depend on many things, including an end to capitalism, but the relationship between sexism and capitalism will not be gone into in this paper. I want to concentrate here on the fact that an end to sex roles requires the equal sharing of childcare by men and women. Only if the pattern of childcare is completely changed can the mass of women be free. There are many other, and equally important, aspects to the feminist struggle—women's control over their own bodies, women's gaining of political and economic power, women's rediscovery of their creativity and sexuality, the end to sexist ideology and attitudes—but the achievements of all these will be limited for the mass of women without the proper sharing of childcare between men and women.

Only when men are constrained/benefited by daily and close association with children will women's potentialities cease to be confined and limited by children. The importance of the childcare issue is demonstrated by the character of anti-feminist arguments, which are based not so much these days on female incapacity or inferiority but on the notion that women must devote themselves primarily to the care of children and of men, and only secondarily to society at large. Further, one of the main barriers to many women's acceptance of feminist ideas is their feeling that in practice their children must come first. And the notion that caring for young children is not a fit occupation for men is extraordinarily deepseated in both men and women. The childcare issue, then, is the structural base of the feminist revolution in the same way as the common ownership of the means of production is of the socialist revolution or the abolition of state power of the anarchist revolution.

Let me make it clear that I do not simply mean men doing an equal share of what women now do—i.e. a creation of househusbands or full-time fathers in equal numbers to housewives and full-time mothers. Nor, obviously, am I talking about the creation of the greater availability of childcare serviced only by women—more female-staffed childcare centres or the extension and rationalisation of backyard child-minding. I mean the finding of new systems of childcare altogether, where there is communal care of various kinds—professional or unprofessional childcare centres and situations—which men run equally with women. I also mean a change in the relation of work to home, so that all adults, whether parents or not, have the opportunity to spend part of their working week in the care of children, and to be paid for it. Such a system will require, among other things, a vast ideological change among men, so that they are forced to abandon the ideology of sexism, and so that they cease to see childcare (along with housework) as inevitably and biologically women's work.

It would seem obvious that feminists want a non-sexist society, and that a non-sexist society requires the equal sharing of children by men and women. But in fact the women's movement does not find this quite so obvious as it should. In practice, a concern with the social reorganisation of childcare is low on the movement's list of priorities and confined to that part of the movement represented by the Women's Electoral Lobby. There is talk of housework and wages for housework, or alternatively the socialisation of housework through communal laundries, eating places, and the like. But much of this discussion misses the point that housework is usually only a real problem and a real burden where there are children or other dependants such as invalids or the very old. Able-bodied adults, whether singly, in couples, or in groups, can, with sufficient labour-saving devices, out-of-home services and a sufficiently simple lifestyle, combine housework with other activities reasonably well. In this circumstance, getting men to do housework is an ideological and not a structural problem. It is childcare that creates the full-time housewife, and it is the problem of childcare rather than housework that requires a fundamental solution. 'Wages for childcare' is a more practical and more revolutionary demand than 'wages for housework'.

There seem to me to be two closely related reasons for the women's movement's relative neglect of the problem of childcare. One is that for most women who become feminists who do not already have children, the present family structure is so oppressive to women that the best personal solution seems to be to not have children. This is a very valid position to take, and is the one taken by most of my friends in the movement. Thus for these women, and for myself until recently, childcare seems to be not their problem. Our present social organisation is such that for most people without children, children become a totally alien segment of society with whom they have little contact, and with whom they can often feel aloof and embarrassed. Thus even should they see the importance of the childcare issue theoretically, they feel helpless to do anything about it. Some way must be found to overcome this helplessness and disinclination, for until the childcare issue is solved, the feminist revolution will be severely hampered and continually jeopardised.

It is up to the women's movement to attack the problem, for if we leave it to men it will never be solved. For all the talk of the joys of parenthood, men do not find childcare sufficiently enjoyable to seize it for themselves. They will have to have it forced upon them. Yet there is in fact a quiet social revolution going on in which men are playing a greater part in the care of children outside working hours. Elizabeth and John Newson demonstrated this in Britain with their study of childcare patterns in Nottingham,[1] and I would say a similar thing is happening here. The crux of the matter, however, the care of children by men *during* 'working hours', is not being solved, for there is no structure within which it can happen. In so far as it is happening—fathers of young children doing part-time jobs and part-time (or even full-time) childcare—it is confined to the professional middle classes. For the male industrial and white-collar working class and for the male employing and managerial capitalist class, daily childcare is as much not-their-business as ever.

This relation of men to childcare brings me to my second reason for the movement's failure to come to grips with the structurally basic problem of childcare. This is the attraction of the view that feminists ought to sever their connections with patriarchal society, and men, altogether. By this argument, women cannot become whole persons as long as they have sexual relations with men. The only personal solution is the celibate or lesbian one, and the only political solution becomes lesbian separatism. The best protagonist for this view is Jill Johnston in her book *Lesbian Nation*.[2] I'll quote from her at some length, for she represents this view very powerfully. She writes (p. 174):

> After there are proper childcare centres and free abortions and easy
> contraception and equal pay and representation and job
> opportunities—then what? There'll still be a man. And biology is
> definitely destiny. The woman in relation to the man historically
> has always been defeated. Every woman who remains in sexual
> relation to man is defeated every time she does it with the man
> because each single experience for every woman is a re-enactment of
> the primal one where she was invaded and separated and fashioned

into a receptacle for the passage of the invader ... If radical feminism is addressing itself to the 'total elimination of sex roles' while still talking sex in relation to the man who defines these roles in the sex act by a certain historical biological-cultural imperative they are going in circles of unadulterated contradictory bullshit ... Feminists who still sleep with the man are delivering their most vital energies to the oppressor. To work out a suitable compromise or *apparent* equality, at any private level, is an exceptional solution between exceptional people ... A personal solution or exceptional adjustment to a political problem is a collusion with the enemy. The solution is getting it together with women. Or separatism ... With her [the lesbian's] consciousness that she alone has no vested interest in prevailing cultural forms she finds that she must struggle within her sexual peer group to create wholly new non-hierarchical modes of interactive behaviour ...

What Jill Johnston is saying is that biology is not, as most feminists would argue, relevant only in the meaning society gives it. The biological differences, she says, *of themselves* amount to inequality and oppression, and will always do so. Take this passage (p. 181):

Biology is not simply ancient or primaeval history. Biology is right now. One can observe the constant renewal of biological imperatives creating their novel if always patriarchal forms of cultural oppression. It is impossible to disentangle biology and culture. The cultural takeover of the male is biologically motivated.

Thus, if biology *is* destiny, women can only become safe and whole by relating sexually to women and not to men.

This view is a compelling one in many ways. It seems convincing that as long as women remain within male-defined institutions such as the family, their revolutionary fervour must be continually compromised by their daily experience and by the continuing chances of finding approval for playing some kind of 'proper' role in the male-defined world. How can you defeat the enemy if you are at the same time seeking his respect and approval? Only the radical lesbians can provide a pure conscience for women as a whole, for only they have forgone all chance of patriarchal approval and cooption.

But such a view is in fact shortsighted and, in the end, authoritarianly prescriptive. First, it is a reversion to the old media-propounded idea that it is not the sexist system which feminists oppose, but the entire class of human beings which is male ('man-hating'). It contains no notion that men as individuals or as a group can change or that in the long run they might have anything to gain from change. It eliminates men entirely from the utopia. Second, it does not have any clear notion of reproduction, of children, and especially of male children. Third, in its extreme form it substitutes for authoritarian patriarchal heterosexuality a new authoritarian homosexuality, prescribing for women their sexual orientation. In being so clear-eyed about means, it loses sight of ends, or defines ends that are actually unrelated for many women, for whom the daily involvement with men and children will continue. It is true that for the heterosexual woman there is an essential contradiction—between her feminist perspectives and ideals and the reality of her involvement in a patriarchal world. She is always being compromised and seduced away from her ideals. But the existence of a contradiction does not imply that the lesbian-separatist solution is *the* solution for all women. Rather it means that non-lesbian feminists must face the problems common to all revolutionaries in a western capitalist society—the gap between ideals and reality, the sense of the impossibility of bringing about profound change, the sense that one's opposition to the system is foiled by the mere process of living within it.

Somehow the women's movement must find a mode of transitional practice, a program for change which attacks immediate problems immediately, and which is such that it contains within it the seeds of profound structural change. This must be true of all activities for the liberation of women. It must be true in particular of actions designed to reform and revolutionise our patterns of childcare. We must cease to indulge in super-feminist notions of men as inferior human beings (only another form of racism, after all), and instead see men as people who must be persuaded or forced to share in the social care of children. I cannot immediately see how this is to be done, but probably it involves the establishment of a strong childcare movement, as a subsidiary or offshoot of the women's movement, with revolutionary aims, devoted to the breakdown of existing work patterns and the establishment of communal childcare. The breakdown of existing work patterns is probably a major threat to capitalist relations of production, and the diversion of sufficient resources to the setting up of adequate and good childcare centres is almost as great a problem. Even though the labour resources used in such centres are more than compensated by the release of more female work-hours in non-childcare work, Australian capitalism just does not seem to see it that way. Above all, a movement for the revolutionising of childcare must be working-class as well as middle-class, with links with the trade union movement, especially the women's trade union movement. When working-class women are fighting to create non-sexist communal childcare, then our feminist revolution will be well on its way.

5

'Damned Whores and God's Police'

It was to be Anne Summers who wrote the feminist revision of Australian history I'd argued for in 1970. Miriam Dixson, Beverley Kingston, and Edna Ryan and Anne Conlon wrote other versions of it. Anne Summers arrived in Sydney from Adelaide in 1971, determined to write a general book about women in Australia. The book came out in 1975, appropriately International Women's Year. Her copy to me is inscribed thus: 'To Ann, I owe you a special debt: your Arena article in 1970 got me started on this . . .' Anne went on to become a well-known journalist, and, for a two-year period, director of the Federal Government's Office for the Status of Women.

When the book came out, I agreed to review it for the ABC radio program 'Books and Ideas'. I recorded the review on 18 November 1975, just a week after the dismissal of the Prime Minister, Gough Whitlam.

1975

Anne Summer's book, *Damned Whores and God's Police: The Colonisation of Women in Australia*, is a landmark for Australian women. It is a landmark in several ways: as a sociological analysis of the situation of women in Australia today, as a feminist critique of Australian culture, and as a frontal attack on sexism in our society. It is also significant for a study of Australian history, and it is as a work of history that I wish to talk about it tonight.

Five of the fourteen chapters are explicitly historical, and the argument contained in them is as follows: women in Australia have always been viewed by men, and often by women themselves, through two competing stereotypes: women are either 'damned whores', or 'God's police'—that is, good wives and mothers guarding the morality and stability of the community as a whole. For the first 50 years of white settlement, women were a small minority, and were almost all considered to be in the former category—'damned whores'. For the remainder of our history, the 'God's police' role has gained ascendancy. The 'damned whores' category, however, has continued to be applied to a minority.

In the convict era, women were consciously and deliberately imported to service the sexual needs of the men, and because of the lack of alternative opportunities either as labourers or as dependent wives, had little option but to conform to the stereotype. This situation ended with the cessation of convict transportation, when it became clear that the new societies in Australia would be based on free labour and require an increased and continuing population. With the desire for economic expansion and social stability came the realisation that the Australian colonies needed above all wives and mothers, rather than whores. Colonial reformers such as Caroline Chisholm emphasised the need, through planned emigration schemes, to increase the number of women in the colonies. They had a strong belief in the importance of women for the creation of a good society, and in the virtues of marriage and the family. The availability of private housing and relatively high wages for men facilitated the establishment of family life.

From the 1860s family life became the dominant pattern and there was much consideration of the details of the particular kind of family on which Australia would be based. The 1890s saw a marked decline in the birthrate, as the preference for smaller families developed. Women themselves now argued that as the size of the family decreased, the quality of family life could increase, especially if women were to be better trained to fill their maternal role. From the 1880s women, especially single women, did enter the workforce, but the notion that they were ultimately to be full-time wives and mothers was enshrined in the basic-wage decisions of the early twentieth century. The Arbitration Court agreed with employers that women should be paid lower wages than men, on the argument that whereas men had to support a family, working women usually supported only themselves.

From the 1880s there developed a feminist movement, and in particular the struggle for women's right to vote. The suffrage movement was essentially middle-class, and stemmed from a combination of factors: the realisation by women that they had no political voice even on matters that most concerned them, such as legislation relating to the family; the realisation by propertied women that they experienced taxation but not representation; and the feeling that if working-class men could vote then so should middle-class women.

The feminists did not attack the family itself, or the idea of a sexual division of labour, though they did argue that women should have options other than motherhood open to them. Their argument was essentially what we would now call 'different but equal', and rested on the notion that women's contribution to society was primarily through their maternal role. In their opposition to the double standard of sexual morality, they were not advocates of sexual freedom: rather than argue that women enjoy the same sexual freedom as men, the feminists wanted men to acquire the same degree of chastity they believed women to be blessed with.

The feminist movement split during the First World War, some using their notion of women's special role to support the war, and others using the same notion to oppose it. During the 1920s women continued to function mainly as homemakers, with their rate of entry into the paid workforce slowing down and the marriage rate continuing to rise. There was no sexual revolution, and socially active women were mainly concerned to combat prostitution, venereal disease, and alcohol. The Depression, which had such a profound effect on Australia, meant that while many men were in forced idleness, suffering great loss of personal status and loss of function, women were either working for very low wages, or working harder than ever in the home to provide for the family on little money. World War II quickly followed, during which women entered the workforce in large numbers, gained wider experiences, more independence, and better pay than they had ever done before.

Yet it was at all times clear that when the war ended the status quo would be resumed, with women returning to the home and men to their jobs. The historical account in the book ends with a description of the retreat to the suburbs of the fifties and sixties, and the growing realisation by women, from the late sixties, that the role of wife and mother could no longer be sufficient. The ideology of 'a woman's place is in the home' continued, while the reality changed with increasing numbers of married women entering the workforce. The rapid suburban spread resulted finally in the dissatisfied suburban housewife, or the woman who was both housewife and paid worker, with conflicting notions about her proper role in life.

The account of the history of the social role of Australian women given by Anne Summers is an extremely useful one, integrating diverse studies of Australia's past—of education, the struggle for the right of women to vote, Australian demographic patterns, the changes in ideas about sexual morality, the great crises of this century. It will enable women to acquire knowledge of their own

activities in the past, and for Australian men to realise that their beliefs about what kind of society Australia is and was are really
beliefs only about the male portion of that society. It will serve to
demonstrate that what feminists are now talking about is not
something superficial or ephemeral, but that Australia has, and has
always had, a sexist social structure which unnecessarily confines
the potential of both sexes and is particularly oppressive to women.
The book, together with other recent feminist writings, demonstrates that feminists are capable, both intellectually and practically, of challenging the sexist status quo.

In all these respects Anne Summers' book reflects the strength
and vitality of the women's movement. Yet the movement has
weaknesses as well as strengths. It remains largely white and
middle-class, not because its members want it to be that way—the
vast majority do not—but because the realities of ethnic and class
division have proved too great. Further, while the movement has
provided a sustained challenge to sexist ideology and attitudes, it
has been less successful in challenging the basic social structures
which reinforce and validate those attitudes. It has been particularly unable to confront the question of creating alternative systems
of childcare, systems in which men would play as significant a role
as women do. Although feminists talk about abolishing the bourgeois family, they have no clear alternative to it. This is because
there is no clear analysis of the family as a unit which, rather than
being isolated from society, is, in social and economic terms, a part
of it. In historical terms, the work done by women within the family
must be analysed in relation to the other kinds of work, paid work,
done outside it.

Anne Summers' book to some extent reflects the weaknesses of
the women's movement in coming to terms with these problems. As
the very title of the book proclaims, it is concerned more with
ideology than with social structure. There is relatively little emphasis in the historical analysis on the structure of the relations between
capital and labour as they particularly affect women. The effects of
a sexual division of labour on the Australian labour movement are
not well discussed. There is little attention to the fact that women
were poor unionists because of their own perception of their role, or
to the ways male unionists concentrated on preserving their rights
against women rather than seeking economic justice for all workers
regardless of sex. The feminists of the 1890s and later are shown to
have been middle-class, but there is only a cursory discussion of the
attitude to them of both the labour movement and of middle-class
male politicians.

Yet one cannot expect one book to do everything. Nor need it do
so, for Anne Summers' book is not an isolated work but rather one
among a number of books now appearing which represents a

feminist challenge to Australian historiography. The study of women at work which *Damned Whores and God's Police* glosses over to some extent is provided by two books recently published by Nelson. *My Wife, My Daughter, and Poor Mary Ann* by Beverley Kingston, focuses on women as workers in the past—as housewives, domestic servants, and as factory, office, and professional workers. It shows that women were not a homogeneous group, but were divided in the work they did according to their class and marital status. *Gentle Invaders*, by Edna Ryan and Anne Conlon, is also a history of women at work in Australia, and especially of the reasons for the very much lower wages women received.

Finally, Anne Summers' book is essentially, though not entirely, about white women. Recent political developments, both at the Women and Politics conference, and at the International Women's Year conference in Mexico, show the importance of black and white women, or Third World and western women, understanding why their aims appear to be so divergent. In Australia black women feel that white women have no real problem, while white women wish that black women would agree that there are certain common problems. This divergence needs to be explored further, and an historical understanding of the issues would be of great benefit. In particular, an understanding of the sexist attitudes and structures of white society which confined white women can help explain the rape, prostitution, deprivation of productive economic role, and necessity for immense personal strength, of Aboriginal women.

This is not the subject of Anne Summers' book. There are still few, if any, studies which seek to analyse the common and divergent experiences of Australian women across racial and ethnic lines.

These reflections are not offered so much as criticisms of what is a very fine and original book, as ideas about where historical and other analysis should go next. For the present, *Damned Whores and God's Police* will do much to deepen our understanding of the history of Australian women.

6

The emergence of a feminist labour history

During 1975 I also reviewed My Wife, My Daughter, and Poor Mary Ann *and* Gentle Invaders. *I had early in the year joined the Labour History group based at ANU, and had become involved in co-editing with Susan Eade (Magarey) and Peter Spearritt a special issue of their journal, on women and work in Australian history.*

I wrote the following review essay as a chapter for this edition. The essay continues the argument for the centrality of the childcare issue that I'd advanced in earlier essays. My insistence on this issue did not derive from my own experience in one sense: John and I shared the childcaring equally, rigidly equally. But this insistence was surely related to my own experience in another sense: I had experienced personally the tension between childcaring and other work.

The collection was reprinted once and is now again out of print. It was, for Labour History, *a considerable success, revealing the very wide and eager readership the feminist movement had attracted by the mid-1970s.*

1975

Australian society will cease to oppress women in particular only when women are capable of achieving a far-reaching change in its structure, and only, therefore, when they can persuade or force men to participate in such a change. Fundamental to the required structural change is a reorganisation of labour which would abolish its sexual division. This means that women and men must not occupy different and unequal places in that part of the workforce which is at present paid, and also that the work of childcare and housekeeping must be shared equally between them. Further, domestic labour must cease to be set apart from the rest of the work done in society: childcare and housework must be made social and communal rather than isolated activities. It is the task of discovering how to achieve this reorganisation of labour while maintaining and extending close personal relationships that now confronts us.[1] Success does not seem possible outside the context of a general social revolution ending capitalism as a social and economic system in Australia.

Our task of sexual and age desegregation will be easier if we understand just how unnecessary, damaging, and historically specific is our present organisation of human labour. The situation of man-breadwinner and woman-childcarer/housewife is not a 'natural', inevitable, or permanent one. Only childbearing is inevitably the province of women: the rest is what human society makes it. Yet the sexual division of labour is a feature of nearly all human societies. If it is to be ended it is necessary to understand just why this is so, and in particular why and how it is so in Australia. The beginnings of this latter understanding are now emerging as the result of the continuing impact of the women's movement on the study of Australian history.

At the time the women's movement began its massive revitalisation in Australia in late 1969, the situation was grim. With the decline in feminist organisation and consciousness after World War II, a generation or so of women had grown up and entered the new women's movement of the early seventies with little knowledge of their past, as women or as feminists. For those of us specifically interested in Australian history, we found that we had been taught little or nothing of the history of women, or of the relations between women and men in all their public and private, political, economic, and social aspects. We had no past—or so, at first, we thought.

We had, of course, a greater written past than we knew. In 1970, when discussing the treatment of women in Australian historical writing, I mentioned the works of Ian Turner, Robin Gollan, Manning Clark, and Russel Ward—all male and all important historians—but I omitted to mention those women who had already written something about women in Australian history. In this omission I was even more indoctrinated than I realised by my male-dominated profession, a profession where not only was the study of women largely ignored, but so too were the women historians who had earlier attempted to undertake that study. My omission was partially redressed by Anne Summers, in her bibliographical essay on Australian women in the first issue of *Refractory*

Girl in 1972.[2] There she discussed various works, including those of Eve Pownall and others on rural 'pioneer' women, the 'feminist-heroic' collections which appeared in the 1930s celebrating the historical 'advance' of women in South Australia, Victoria, and New South Wales, the biography of Caroline Chisholm by Margaret Kiddle, and an article by Dianne Scott on the Australian women's suffrage movement.[3] She suggested that these works were useful, though in various ways limited, contributions towards a history of Australian women.

One of these works, by Eve Pownall, has recently been reissued by Rigby under the new title *Australian Pioneer Women*. Her book is the story of the 'first white women', the women on the frontiers of rural settlement, the women who, in fact, represented the permanency of Aboriginal dispossession. It is also the story of rural women at work. She aims to show that white pioneer women engaged not only in housekeeping, childbearing, and childrearing, bringing comfort and continuity where otherwise there was none, but worked also at 'the growing and harvesting of the first crops, the establishment of the sheep industry, [and] the setting up of cattle stations'.

Pownall describes the life of many different rural women. Aboriginal women in traditional society were economically important ('her foraging was the main food supply for her mate and family'), and they carried out, as did white women, the work of childbearing and childrearing. When the whites came, Aboriginal women 'performed "domestic and sexual duties" and acted as a link between the settlers and the tribe'. They assisted white women with simple remedies, as nursemaids to white children, and frequently as emergency midwives. Pownall then goes on to describe the work of the convict women as domestic servants and prostitutes, and the farming and childrearing work of early women settlers in New South Wales. The story of the women settlers is repeated for colonial expansion over the whole continent. White women performed domestic labour, ran the dairies and the barnyards, frequently worked as shepherds, and supplied pastoral labour when the white male labour went to the goldfields. German women were active in the earliest productive agriculture in South Australia, and supplied the first shearers for the colony. Pownall's method is to describe the lives of individual women; she writes of Sarah Durack in Queensland:

> Clearing and sowing, yarding and branding, with Sarah doing her share in the fields, her baby lain to sleep in a freshly turned furrow. Then home to cook and bake, scrub and mend, her washing done so late that the night was nearly gone when she finished and crept into bed without disturbing her sleeping husband. (p. 210.)

Pownall then rounds out her picture of women at work with chapters on the early nurses, the first women doctors, and unpaid (but financially secure) social workers such as Caroline Chisholm, Catherine Helen Spence, and Mary Windeyer.

Pownall's account of the early female white settlers is a useful, and interesting, and well-illustrated one, though there is an unresolved tension between her sympathy for Aboriginal society, with the status and security it afforded women, and her tendency to glorify the settlement process which destroyed much of that society. Yet the hardships of white pioneer women were real enough, and in her evocation of these hardships she shows the rural white women truly at work. She offers little interpretation in her account; she could, for example, have made the point more explicitly that women were used in rural areas as a reserve labour force. Where there was a shortage of labour women were used in non-domestic tasks, and promptly returned to domestic tasks when the shortage eased through the use of Aboriginal labour and the introduction of such measures as fencing. Where a labour shortage continued— especially in agriculture and in the sheep and cattle runs of the poor selectors—women continued to carry out non-domestic tasks. Eve Pownall's book, though largely impressionistic and unexplanatory, was nevertheless itself in 1959 a pioneering effort. Its reissue is very welcome.

The present women's movement has at last resulted in a new wave of writing on the history of Australian women at work, and this time the emphasis is urban. This is reflected not only in this present volume of essays. Beverley Kingston's book, *My Wife, My Daughter, and Poor Mary Ann* analyses the situation of women across class and marital lines. The strength of her book lies in the connections and contrasts she draws between these varied conditions—women single or married, women working for money or for 'love'. She begins with the well-off middle-class married women. Until the 1920s or 1930s such women had four tasks: the bearing and often the rearing of children (there were few nannies), the overseeing of their domestic servants, the provision of 'society' whereby status, caste, and hierarchy were maintained in subtle social ways, and very often unpaid humanitarian or social work, for hospitals, schools, churches, and 'homes' and hostels of various kinds. Some were engaged as social and moral watchdogs in organisations such as the Women's Christian Temperance Union, while others were active in the struggle for the franchise. With the decline in the availability of servants throughout the twentieth century, public activity by middle-class women became more difficult, as they were forced back into the home to do most, if not all, their housework and childcare themselves.

Kingston also discusses the situation of the less well-off married woman, the housewife without domestic servants. The hope of marriage was what made single life bearable, but for the housewife there was in the twentieth century a loss of challenge, skill, and training. Yet there was also a reduction in heavy domestic labour with the introduction of gas, electricity, and plumbing. With the easier domestic burden and smaller families, the idea that married women could work outside the home as well as in it gained some currency in the 1920s, but ended with the Depression, to be replaced by ideals of femininity and glamour. The ideology of 'woman's place' ensured that labour-saving devices did not secure the housewife's emancipation from the home.

Domestic service was the original paid labour for unmarried girls and women, and by 1901 was still the occupation of almost half the paid female labour force. Yet even by the 1870s supply did not match demand, and the decline in the availability of domestic servants continued, hastened by World War I, and especially by the Depression and World War II. This occurred essentially because single women preferred factory work, with its company, shorter and better regulated hours, and better pay. Domestic service, Kingston graphically shows, was marked by loneliness, tyranny and supervision, sheer hard physical work, very long hours, and low pay. Domestic servants were virtually impossible to unionise, the peak in attempts at their unionisation occurring in the first decade of the twentieth century.

Female entry into factory work increased as factories increased in the latter part of the nineteenth century. This process reached a peak in 1911, when 28.42 per cent of the industrial workforce was female, declined in the 1920s and 1930s, and returned to its 1911 level with World War II. The interwar decline was matched, however, by women's entry into occupations associated with health, education, and commerce. Most paid women workers were single, few married women being employed until the 1930s, and they worked in predominantly female industries such as clothing and textiles, and food and drink manufacture. Women's paid work was regarded as a temporary phase in their lives, preceding marriage. That it was so regarded by women led to their poor unionisation, and that it was so regarded by employers and the state led to their being paid low wages, on the grounds that they, unlike men, were not breadwinners. While their wages remained low, attempts were made to improve their conditions by benevolent liberal patriarchal bodies, such as the New South Wales Royal Commission of 1911, which expressed concern about the health and morality of factory women. Kingston concludes with a chapter on the position of the unmarried woman, to whom society gave no respect, recognition, or concern. Increasing numbers entered the workforce as low-paid workers, as their previous role of unpaid housekeeper in their

father's family was made redundant by the reduction of the
domestic labour burden. Their social position worsened with the
popularisation of Freud, for now their earlier moral strength was
seen as sexual unfulfilment and inadequacy.

Kingston's book establishes the outlines of Australian women's
work, and therefore of their social roles. The degree of detail
devoted to particular areas varies enormously. Compare, for
example, the detailed and fascinating discussion of what housework
was like before and after the advent of gas and electricity, with the
lack of demonstration of the frequently repeated assertion that the
popularisation of Freud diminished respect for the single woman.
Or contrast the vivid discussion of the working conditions of nurses
in the nineteenth and early twentieth centuries with the generality
and vagueness of the discussion of how the concept of the family
wage was used to pay very low wages to women. But these are
cranky criticisms, and Kingston wards them off in her introduction,
where she says she 'made a decision to press on as soon as a
coherent outline had become clear'.

But there are two criticisms which are perhaps not so unimport-
ant. One is that in her disdain for the study of Australian race
relations, through her notion that such a study is an indulgence in
'interesting minorities', a byway that avoids the mass of ordinary
women, Kingston has unnecessarily limited her interpretative
framework. For what was this process of 'building a modern and
progressive society in a new land far from its origins' of which she
writes? None other than the colonisation of Australia itself, the
superimposition, at great human costs, on Aboriginal Australia of a
British community. The hard work done by white women that she
describes so well was the underbelly of the colonising enterprise.
The connections between colonisation and the oppression of
women are important. Carmel Shute's remarks in *Hecate* are
salutary in this connection:

> The oppression of women is closely interwoven with notions of race.
> In Australia, which is a tiny enclave of white settlement isolated in
> the Pacific, the desire for a high birthrate and the maintenance of
> racial strength and purity have long been national priorities
> ... Concomitant with the cry to 'populate or perish', the decimation
> and containment of Aborigines and the exclusion and restriction of
> non-white immigrants, has been the confinement of women to their
> reproductive functions. White women in Australia have been viewed
> primarily as breeders of the Anglo-Saxon strain ... [4]

To look at it another way, when the study which Kingston rightly
recommends of prostitution in Australia is done, it will not be able
to ignore Aboriginal women, one of those 'interesting minorities'.
Perhaps it is her urban emphasis which enables Kingston to ignore

Aboriginal society so completely, for in a rural study the interconnections between sexual and racial exploitation would (or should) be impossible to ignore.

The other doubt is raised by the near absence in the book of a discussion of the work of childcare, one of the most arduous, time-consuming, skilled, housework-producing, and exclusively female of labour activities done by women. She does mention the state's interest in a high birthrate, but has only a very short discussion (on p.108) of the work of childrearing itself. There she makes the point that where childcare was once 'a matter of instinct and family lore handed on from mother to daughter', by the 1920s or so this method of training had been jeopardised by social and geographic mobility and by new psychological theory. Governments intervened with regulations on the quality of food given to children, and then with baby health clinics. Yet the detail given so well elsewhere is missing here, and more seriously, the importance of the work of childbearing to a theoretical understanding of women's labour in general is not seen. For example, she suggests that in the 1930s or thereabouts labour-saving devices did not free women for full entry into the life of the society because of 'all the mythology and shibboleths about a woman's power and a woman's place'. This is only a partial answer; an allied and more fundamental one is that labour-saving devices do not mind children. While technology reduced the burden of heavy household labour, it did not alter the isolated character of childcare.

Edna Ryan and Anne Conlon's *Gentle Invaders: Women at Work in Australia, 1788–1974* is rather different. Where Kingston is primarily concerned with the conditions of women's work, and the social position surrounding it, Ryan and Conlon are really concerned with women's wages. They emphasise two important and related questions: first, along with Kingston, the segregation of men and women in the labour market, and second, the low wages paid to women. They begin with the British background, showing that industrialisation led to increasing segregation, breaking down the family-based rural work pattern. The women who entered the workforce for wages were usually single, and were employed in textile and clothing industries and in domestic service. Australia continued the British pattern of sex segregation at work. Up to about 1860 most paid women were domestic servants, but after 1860 they increasingly entered factories, especially clothing factories. Factory Acts in the 1880s and 1890s sought to prevent sweated labour and outwork. Employers and unions both ensured that women were kept out of 'men's work' and confined to predominantly female industries and to the lowest grades of work within an industry. Despite low pay, women's participation in the workforce increased steadily from 1900; women were less hard hit by the Depression, and began working in increasing numbers during World War II.

Women's wages were throughout conditioned by the fact that it was assumed that men were the breadwinners, and that paid working women had no dependants. Government intervention in wage-fixing in Australia was extremely important, and based on this principle. In 1907 the Harvester judgment of a Commonwealth Arbitration Court judge, Justice Higgins, with its concept of the 'living wage', was based on this family wage concept. Another Arbitration Court judgment in 1912 further stated that equal pay could only be granted in 'men's industries', in order to protect male workers from cheap female labour, and should not be granted in 'women's industries', where men did not have to be protected. By 1918 the court agreed to a female minimum of 50 per cent of the male minimum, and women were also given lower margins for skill.

The fight for equal pay began in the 1930s, in the recovery from the Depression. In 1937 a Council of Action for Equal Pay was established, and in 1940 and 1941 the Australian Council of Trade Unions actively sought equal pay.[5] From 1942 to 1945 the wartime emergency Women's Employment Board set women's wage rates on the basis of a new concept—not need (the 'living wage'), not capacity of industry to pay (the Depression concept), but the efficiency and productivity of women as compared to men. Women were still given lower than the male rate, but it was higher than before, ranging from 75 to 100 per cent of the male rate.[6] In 1945 the government legislated that women could not be paid less than 75 per cent of the male minimum.

The gains made during the war were partially but not wholly lost later. In 1949 the Commonwealth Arbitration Court reverted to the breadwinner concept, and awarded women 75 per cent of the male minimum plus lower (junior) margins for skill. Since that time women have very gradually achieved equal pay. Equal pay for equal (that is, identical and easily comparable) work was granted in principle in New South Wales in 1959, teachers gaining it in practice in 1963, and by the Commonwealth in 1969. An adverse result of this principle was that it encouraged employers to further segregate work. The real breakthrough came in 1970 in the Commonwealth Arbitration Court's decision for the metal trades, which allowed one rate for the job. All workers under federal awards were granted this in 1972, and in 1974 the female minimum wage was brought level with the male minimum. The only employer escape now was to underclassify the jobs women did. The present situation appears to be that while women continue to fill the lower-paid jobs, they cannot be paid less on the 'breadwinner' argument.

Ryan and Conlon's book is a valuable account of how women came to be paid low wages for so long, and of how sex segregation in the workforce ensured and continues to ensure that their wages are generally lower than men's. Their book does, however, by implication and omission, reinforce the notion that it is paid work that is somehow real and valuable, and that unpaid work (childcare and housework) is secondary, of little importance to the Australian economy. Further, they do not draw out the connections between unpaid and paid labour, missing, like Kingston, the central role of childbearing to women's situation in the workforce. They treat the 'male breadwinner' concept largely as a fiction, emphasising the fact that many women were also breadwinners, their low wages reducing them and their dependants to levels of extreme poverty. Important as the exceptions were, the fact remains that most men were breadwinners and most women were not. They are on surer ground when they say that the concept defined women's proper place as in the home. Ultimately, wage equality is essential not only for the full respect and financial independence of women, but also for the possibility of reorganising all labour, including housework and childcare, along non-sexist lines.

Gentle Invaders is full of valuable information, but it is not always clearly presented. There is a mass of statistics offered, all fascinating in themselves, but frequently unrelated to and non-comparable with one another, so that the picture of the nature and rate of women's entry into the paid workforce is rather confused.[7] On one aspect of the situation, that of sex segregation at work, a much clearer and more concise account is given for the post-1911 period by Margaret Power in her recent article, 'The Making of a Woman's Occupation'.[8] Power clearly demonstrates that industrialisation, the relative and absolute increase in the female workforce, and increased education for women, have not reduced this segregation. Female occupations are still 'those in which work relationships between women and men are analogous to the subservient position of women in the household' and in society at large. She goes on to show that some occupations become increasingly segregated as men occupy the higher positions (as in nursing, social work and librarianship), and that others, because of the social inequality of men and women, switch their sex identity rather than be composed equally of men and women. Her weakest discussion is in her policy recommendations, for here she stresses piecemeal change (what to do when an occupation seems about to switch its sex) rather than those fundamental changes in attitudes and economic and social institutions upon which she merely touches.

The research for the three books discussed was undertaken before the current outbreak of theoretical work, mainly marxist and mainly non-Australian, on the family and its relation to the organisation of labour in capitalist society.[9] Future work in Australian women's labour history will have to take into account the new theoretical insights, so that the economic and social value of women's unpaid labour and the central role of that labour in women's total social labour is better understood. Nevertheless, despite the difficulties and weaknesses and the fact that so much remains to be done, the works discussed are already forming a picture of the history of women's work in Australia. Although, as the example of Margaret Power's article demonstrates, clear analysis does not of itself necessarily yield the best proposals for change, the kind of knowledge and understanding of women's work that is now emerging will greatly assist the feminist assault on the sexual division of labour in Australia.

7

Women's studies

Feminism enters the academy

The period between 1971 and 1975 had been a productive one for Australian feminist scholarship. Not only had several books been written, but the journals Refractory Girl *(Sydney) and* Hecate *(Brisbane) had been established. Furthermore, there emerged a movement demanding courses on women's studies in the universities and colleges. Some of this demand was for courses based within existing departments, most controversially in philosophy at the University of Sydney in 1973. There was also pressure for courses which cut across the usual disciplinary barriers.*

During 1974 there was a major battle at ANU over proposals to set up an interdisciplinary course in women's studies in the School of General Studies, and by the end of the year the school had agreed that such a course should be offered. In June 1975 a conference on women's studies was held in Adelaide. With a six month old baby, I did not go, but I wrote a paper (in response to a discussion sheet sent out to potential conference-goers) for the conference and sent it off. The second half of the paper, printed here, touched on the debate between advocates of inter- or transdisciplinary women's studies, and advocates of feminist scholarship within the disciplines, a debate which was never really resolved.

41

1975

... There are two problems with the view that those who wish to study women, and issues of concern to the women's movement, should opt out of the existing disciplines and into women's studies. One is methodological; the other political. The methodological problem is that while women's studies courses represent a content area, and have perhaps some ideological unity, they do not, and cannot, have methodological coherence. Such coherence can only be achieved within the disciplines, even though these exist ultimately only to be transcended. The political problem is that women's studies, unless it draws from and feeds back into the traditional disciplines, will become an isolated enclave within the university, representing the intellectual ghettoisation of women.

People doing women's studies should therefore also develop and maintain their alignment specifically to one or more disciplines. Further, teachers and students in women's studies courses should put pressure on teachers in the traditional disciplines to raise the 'women's studies' content of their courses, and offer assistance to this end to those who think there are no relevant reading materials available, or no people available to lead discussions. In the teaching of Australian history, for example, there is still hardly any mention of women, a result both of lack of research and reading material, and of the ignorance or opposition of those teaching Australian history courses. Those involved in women's studies, then, need to undertake research and publish their findings, and bring these to the attention of staff teaching history.

Research is essential if we are to be able to provide this necessary reading and resource material. We need people doing research in the framework of traditional disciplines, and still respecting the body of scholarship and method developed within those disciplines. In history, for example, it is still important to respect such things as methods of presenting evidence, indication of sources, narrative and analytical skills, and problems of empiricism versus theoretical generalisation in history. Similarly, in discussing literature by or about women, the traditional skills of literary criticism are still necessary, and the complex problems of literature as a distinct form and literature as part of society, must be entered into. The same points can be made for sociology, politics, psychology, biology, and so on.

If we abandon our access to traditional disciplines we abandon those very skills which help us to develop critiques of existing views about women, and strategies for a genuine feminist revolution.

Notes from the second year

Six months after the Adelaide women's studies conference, I was appointed to teach the women's studies course at the Australian National University. I devised a system whereby there was a general introductory section, discussing sexual biological difference, the reasons for the sexual division of labour, and the public/private dichotomy. This was followed by a series of special topics: the 'new woman' in English fiction; the history of feminist thought, 1790–1977; sex differences and psychological processes; women in Australian society, past and present; capitalism and the family; and women in developing countries. Two more were planned but had to be dropped for lack of student interest: women in Shakespeare and thirteenth-century Italian poetry, and ethics and intersexual relations. I ran the introductory section, and the special topics on feminist thought and on women in Australian society and history, while the other four special topics were taught by tutors, lecturers, and research fellows (male and female) in other departments and schools in the university, none of whom gained any kind of payment or credit for the teaching assistance they gave me. My course, then, combined some interdisciplinary study (e.g. the introductory section, the special topic on capitalism and the family) with some study based on disciplines (e.g. women in Australian history).

They were overall a good two years, for the students were very committed and I was able to develop good relations with and much-needed assistance from various members of staff scattered through the university. Further, it was a valuable time for me in the sense that I was forced to look outside my own discipline, history, much more than I ever had before. In particular, I had to learn the debates over how to understand the position of women that were going on in anthropology and sociology.

There were problems, however: because I was a single-person department, merely 'attached' to a history department, sections of which did not want me to be there, my job was often lonely and exhausting. Although the battle for a women's studies course had been won in 1974, there were many on the staff in the faculty who opposed the concept altogether. One of the most hostile was Professor Zubrycki, of Sociology, who attacked me at a Faculty Board meeting for having Kate Millett's Sexual Politics, not a respectable scholarly work he said, on my reading list. It was because of hostility such as this, and despite the warmth and assistance I encountered from key people, that I had a strong feeling that the program could be abolished at any time. This fear was, however, to prove groundless. The program is still going and, I understand, going well.

At the end of the two years I wrote a piece for Woroni, the ANU student newspaper, reflecting on my experiences. I did not, in the end, submit it for publication.

1977

The women's studies course has now been a fact of ANU existence for two years. From the time in 1974 when it was first demanded right up to the present, its very existence and its purpose and form have been matters of controversy. There are many who see it, variously, as unnecessary, sexist, vague, intellectually invalid, or, for women, self-defeating. There are others who see it as essential, anti-sexist, coherent, challenging, intellectually demanding, and valuable, either as a corrective to the male-centred or sexist nature of much university education, or as a place where the questions thrown up by the women's movement can be aired and examined in depth. It is a course which, while many are still apathetic towards it, has attracted enormous interest and attention. As the convenor of the course, I am constantly asked 'how is the women's studies course going?'.

I am not really the person to answer that question. The answer lies with the students who have taken the course. The only printed student response was by Isabella Martinis in the 1977 Students' Orientation Handbook. She found the course 'academically very rewarding since I now know how to write essays on feminist issues without floundering in revolutionary passion and causing myself embarrassment'. But she found the course in 1976 a failure in that it didn't develop a feminist perspective, in that 'the same old class formats prevailed', and in that women's studies created 'very few ripples'. She concluded that the course should have 'an explicit aim at political effectiveness within the feminist movement as a whole'.

Isabella's response to the course was, as she pointed out, only one of many. Some other students would not have found the lack of a feminist perspective (if there was such a lack) at all a matter for concern; others were more wholehearted in their approval. But Isabella's reactions were, I know, shared by other students. Her positive statements about the course I found heartening, for I consider one of the purposes of a women's studies course to be to assist people to talk and write about women *as women*, in a way that can incorporate the best traditions of intellectual inquiry.

Her criticism of the 'same old class formats' was, I think, justified in relation to the earlier part of the course, though not I think to the later part, or to the course this year. The course has moved very much in the direction of a reliance on student contribution and discussion, though I still feel that staff have an important function in providing a sound structure to any course, in raising issues in lectures, seminars and tutorials, and in assisting students in their reading and essay writing. But these are educational issues which are not confined to women's studies courses.

The questions of a 'feminist perspective', and an explicit aim at political effectiveness, are much more difficult. They are issues which divide students within the course, and can divide staff as well. My own view is that students within the course can derive from it whatever purposes they wish. But the role of staff is necessarily one of allowing for the needs of all students, so long as they are not detrimental to the course as a whole, of providing an arena where differing positions are argued out, and where all participants, staff and students, are forced to clarify and defend their ideas in the light of the available evidence on any particular issue. For this reason I do not believe a women's studies course should have a feminist perspective as such, but rather be a place where feminist perspectives are aired, criticised, examined, and developed.

Thus women's studies courses contribute to the feminist movement not by preaching feminist conclusions (which vary enormously anyway) but by considering seriously the questions feminists raise, and by equipping people to deal with those questions in whatever public, political, personal, or work situations they might concurrently or later encounter.

Women's studies courses necessarily have a number of functions. They contribute to social analysis, philosophical discourse, and historical understanding, and these things are important. For me, to understand the past and present better is important not only for the women's movement, but also for this class-structured, inegalitarian, racist, and sexist society generally. The study of women's history is therefore valuable not only for women, but also for anyone who is seeking to understand social, political, and economic realities.

The impact of the women's studies course on the rest of this university is hard to determine. I never expected it to be enormous; it is one course among hundreds. Some argue that the presence of a women's studies course 'lets other staff off the hook' in relation to the study of women. This may have partly happened, and if it has, all those in the university who care about the study of women must act to correct it, by consistently raising the issue at the departmental and course level. But in fact it seems to me that teaching which focuses on women and gender-related issues has increased in this university in recent years. There need be no conflict between an interdisciplinary women's studies course and departmental single-discipline courses on women. There is a place for both: disciplinary courses to reach students otherwise unaffected and to consider the relationship between gender-related issues and the theoretical and methodological concerns of that discipline, and interdisciplinary women's studies courses to put these various kinds of analyses together and to allow for a concentration on women's studies problems.

The future of the women's studies program at ANU is at this point unclear. It may stabilise, expand, or contract. These options will be considered, and decisions made, in the coming year. Its success will depend on Faculty, staff and student commitment to it. A convenor of a women's studies course has to expect attack from all sides—from the Right and the Left, the feminists and anti-feminists, the women's movement and the university—and in varying degrees I have been so attacked. A women's studies course raises emotional responses that many other courses do not; the bitterness, insecurities and inequalities in the relations between men and women in this society are brought into an arena, the university, which while itself often exemplifying them, also traditionally prefers to stand apart. But ultimately I can only thank all those—staff, and especially students—who have so far contributed to the course, for their enthusiasm, hard work, support, and friendship, and even, at times, for their opposition, hostility, and criticism.

PART III

A tale of two discourses: marxism and feminism

8

Women — a 'reserve army of labour'?

Of all the issues raised by women's liberation and subsequently women's studies, it was that of the relationship between women and work, otherwise expressed as that between the family and capitalism, or reproduction and production, that continued to concern me most, intellectually and politically.

In the debates since 1970, there had been a general acceptance of the notion that women were a reserve army of labour. The 'reserve army of labour' was a concept borrowed from Karl Marx. Marx had used it to analyse the ways in which capitalism relied on pools of unemployed as a basis for keeping wages down. Feminists in the 1970s used it in a more specific sense, to refer to the particular way in which women flowed in and out of the labour market as the economy demanded. I had used the concept myself when I'd criticised Eve Pownall in 1975 for not pointing out that 'women were used in rural areas as a reserve labour force'. Following an American economic historian, Ruth Milkman, I wrote a critique of this notion for a special Canberra issue of Refractory Girl *produced in 1977. Soon afterwards Margaret Power, a lecturer in political economy at the University of Sydney, developed a similar argument, based on more detailed empirical research than I had done.*

1977

The notion that women are used as a 'reserve army of labour', drawn into the economy in times of expansion and wartime and pushed out to a greater extent than men in times of depression and postwar readjustment, has become commonplace in feminist analysis in Australia as it has elsewhere. The 'reserve army' thesis suggests that the existence of two alternative roles for women (paid worker and unpaid full-time housewife) creates a practical and ideological flexibility in women's employment, not available in men's employment, which is very useful to societies whose labour force needs to fluctuate according to economic and wartime conditions.

In a recent paper Bettina Cass wrote: 'Women constitute, and are used as, a "reserve army" of labour in industrial societies . . . In the Australian post-war economy, married women. . . have gained jobs when labour is scarce . . . and they are the first laid off in times of unemployment.' Anne Summers uses the concept several times in *Damned Whores and God's Police:* 'The War [WWII] showed that women could effectively be used as a reserve labour force because once their labour was no longer required they could be returned to the home.' 'In the post-war period . . . the Government realised that the country's women constituted a splendid reserve labour force.' In 'Women, Arbitration and the Family', Penny Ryan and Tim Rowse state that 'Women, especially married women, constitute a "reserve army of the unemployed" ' and that 'when capitalists employing men and women begin retrenchments, they often have the full support of the union in firing women first'.[1]

These are local applications of the 'reserve army' thesis stated by feminist writers elsewhere, including Kate Millett, who speaks in *Sexual Politics* of an economic situation where women are exploited as a reserve labour force, periodically and widely purged from employment, and when reintroduced, confined to its lower reaches.[2]

It may be time to question the accuracy and usefulness of the 'reserve army' thesis. The questioning which follows is based on a perception of certain inconsistencies in the argument itself, and on insights from an article by Ruth Milkman, which sets out to show the inadequacy of the thesis for the United States.[3] In the light of these perceptions and insights, a re-examination of the Australian data on women's unemployment seems vitally necessary, and is argued for, rather than actually attempted, here.

In general, the 'reserve army' thesis obscures the fact that overall, this century, women have fairly steadily entered the workforce, for various reasons including the entry of the functions performed by housewives into the market economy. Fluctuations in this process have been of two kinds: a) times of severe unemployment, which have affected men in ways similar to, and at times worse than, women, and b) times of war and postwar reconstruction in which the sex character of occupations is radically disturbed and then substantially restored. It seems possible that while women are drawn into the paid workforce in times of expansion, they are not expelled in times of contraction to any greater extent than are men, and that war and postwar conditions present a special, though illuminating, case which cannot easily be generalised to peacetime economic conditions.

The reserve army thesis rests on the assumption that female unemployment is relatively acceptable, to employers and workers alike. But how acceptable can female unemployment be to that large part of the working class which has always and increasingly depended on the earnings of women? Are, perhaps, the demands that women be sacked first based more on the middle-class professional and skilled workers whose higher salaries and wages reduce dependence on women's paid labour? And how anxious are employers to sack their cheapest workers? How, in practice, are the competing considerations of women's cheaper labour and men's greater ability to press their right to employment worked out? If the workforce is as sex-segregated as it is, how often does the choice between a male worker and a female worker arise, making it possible to sack women in order to make way for men? Does the sacking of women from men's jobs after World War II really prove the 'reserve army' thesis? If the sacked women went, after some delay, into the expanding 'female' occupations, would not the sacking of women from men's jobs indicate not the validity of the reserve army thesis so much as the fundamental importance of maintaining sex segregation and inequality in the workforce?

These doubts about the reserve army thesis are strengthened by the observation that its exponents do not give substantial statistical or other evidence to support the thesis. This is in marked contrast to the wealth of evidence produced to support other feminist economic analyses, concerning sex segregation in the workforce and sex-based differential levels of income.[4]

Ruth Milkman raises some of these questions in her discussion of women's employment and unemployment in the United States from 1930 to the present. She begins by pointing out that there is a real contradiction in a capitalist economy between the need, on the one hand, for women's unpaid household labour, and the tendency, on the other, to draw all suitable labour power, regardless of sex, into the sphere of production for profit. The continuation of the ideology and practice of the family under these conditions means that women who work for wages are nevertheless viewed, both by themselves and by men, as essentially wives and mothers (real or potential) not as 'workers'. As a result, when jobs are scarce as in the Great Depression of the 1930s, women will be urged to leave the paid labour force to make way for men, the rightful job occupants. Married women, and women in the rare mixed-sex occupations, such as teaching, will be particularly pressured. However, despite these pressures, in the 1930s women did not leave the workforce to make way for men for two reasons: first, the sexual segregation of most occupations created an inflexibility in the labour market which prevented women's expulsion, and second, since this inflexibility meant that the loss of a female job did not entail the gaining of a male job, the withdrawal of women from the workforce was against the material interests of those families where the men were unemployed or poorly paid.

Women's unemployment, in fact, was not as severe as men's, because the predominantly female (clerical, trade and service) occupations declined less than the predominantly male manufacturing occupations. Where women did suffer unemployment, this was because the 'women's jobs' involved were volatile or declining, not because men replaced women. There was no evidence of mobility from male to female occupations, and in fact the degree of sex segregation in the occupational structure increased slightly between 1930 and 1940.

Milkman suggests that it is in their family role, not their paid work role, that women were most profoundly affected by the Depression of the 1930s. Because of the need to reduce expenditure under conditions of unemployment and low wages, women substituted their own labour for goods and services they had formerly purchased in the marketplace. Home food-preserving, home sewing, and similar activities dramatically increased; the long-term trend towards integrating such activities into the sphere of paid labour was temporarily reversed.

Milkman then moves on to discuss women's role in the workforce in World War II and after. She says that between 1940 and 1944 the number of women in the paid workforce increased by 6 million, but by 1946 had been reduced by 4 million from the 1944 level. Women's war jobs were partially handed over to men, and partially eliminated and replaced by male occupations arising from the reconversion to manufacturing industries producing foods for consumption. Women were, however, by the mid-1950s reintegrated into the workforce to the 1944 level through the expanding 'female' white-collar and service occupations.

The concluding section of the article deals with the current economic situation in the USA. Milkman states that now, as in the 1930s, the male labour market has suffered proportionately greater cuts than the female labour market. Sex segregation in the workforce is now, as in the 1930s, the key to understanding sex differences in rates of unemployment in times of economic contraction.

Ruth Milkman's article is persuasive and well documented, though three points need to be elaborated further. First, why did women's occupations suffer less than men's in the 1930s Depression, and are all depressions (and recessions) similar in this respect? Second, what impact did World War II have on women's postwar employment experience? Did any occupations switch from male to female as a result of the war? What is the real cause-and-effect relationship between the temporary decline in women's employment in the immediate postwar years, and the growth in the birthrate of those years? Third, she suggests there are two conflicting attitudes surrounding women's employment in times of crisis: first, that women should not take men's jobs, but second, that women's income is doubly valued at such times. There is a need to look more closely at the situation in non-segregated occupations as compared with segregated ones, and also at the proposition that the ideology of 'a woman's place is in the home' was necessarily stronger among the middle-class and skilled workers than semi- and unskilled workers. That is, the class character of ideologies concerning women's employment needs to be analysed.

A similar analysis to Ruth Milkman's needs to be undertaken for Australia. We already have Anne Summers' work on the 1930s Depression, in which she describes patterns similar to those Milkman finds for the USA.[5] She does not, however, draw out the implications concerning the importance of sex segregation in the workforce, that Milkman does so sharply. The mobilisation of Australian women in World War II has still not been thoroughly examined, and informed discussion of the immediate postwar period is even harder to find. We need to examine further the ideology of women's role at least from the 1930s to the present, along the lines of Andree Wright's study of the *Woman's Weekly*,[6] and more particularly the class and sex differences concerning this ideology. Finally, the nature of and reasons for current differentials between male and female unemployment need closer examination. Has the extension of equal pay led to a growth in the preferential hiring of men, or is the sex segregation of the workforce sufficient to make equal pay only marginally relevant? What are the differing fortunes of male and female occupations at present?

The importance of this analysis lies in the necessity for feminists to be adequately prepared for any ideological or real changes concerning women's employment. For feminists an understanding of the critical relation between women's paid and unpaid employment is strategically urgent under conditions of high unemployment for both sexes. On the one hand, married women's employment is being and will increasingly be challenged on the usual grounds, and we should examine closely the source of this challenge. On the other hand, women's employment as such, though not its pay or conditions, is at least partially protected by sex segregation in the workforce, by the financial need for women's employment at least among the working class, and by a more general acceptance than existed previously of women's need for and right to paid employment. Any campaign countering attacks on women's paid employment will have to take account of these somewhat contradictory pressures, and direct its attention to the interrelated issues of women's pay, conditions and status while at work, the significance of part-time work in changing employment needs and patterns, and the kind of economy which might guarantee both full employment and the transformation and sex-sharing of childcaring and housework.

9

Explaining the sexual division of labour

After this critique of the feminist use of the marxist concept of a 'reserve army of labour', I wrote very little for publication on women for three years. I had changed jobs, and my new workplace—the School of Humanities and Social Sciences at the New South Wales Institute of Technology—was extremely demanding. But the reasons for my failure to write or develop my ideas further, I think now in retrospect, lay elsewhere. They had to do with what I have referred to earlier as an 'outbreak in theoretical work' on the family and capitalism.

In Australia the years from about 1976 to 1983 were the heyday of the influence of a particular brand of marxism in radical intellectual circles. This was sometimes called structuralist marxism, but more often Althusserian marxism, in recognition of the key role played by the French marxist philosopher Louis Althusser. This was a form of marxism which placed great emphasis on the structure of society under capitalism, and on specifying the relationship between various 'instances' within that structure—the economic, the ideological, the political. It located power very much in the hands of the state, by including within 'the state' not only the political functions we normally think of but also such social institutions as the family, and indeed ideology, the way we think, itself. A key feature of this kind of marxism was also that it distinguished between 'science' and 'ideology', so that ideology became those ideas which inhered in society's dominant structures and which explained why the mass of people accepted a system so patently inegalitarian and destructive as capitalism, while science became those forms of knowledge that were not so embedded. In practice, 'science' often became what the

*Althusserians themselves thought, while 'ideology' became the false
ideas everyone else held.*

It was a view of society that many found exciting for its attempt to
specify rigorously the relationship between different elements in the
social structure, and because it focused on the power of institutions,
which much previous marxism had been neglecting in favour of
vague theories like 'alienation' and 'reification'. It was, we can now
see, very mechanistic, very rigid, very functionalist. Social institutions, or ideologies, were examined for the role they played in
maintaining, 'reproducing', the system of capitalism. It was assumed
that all social institutions and ideologies were functional for capitalism, otherwise either they or capitalism would not exist. It was
indeed a particular intervention in marxist and sociological debates
concerning 'agency' and 'structure', themselves a continuation of
much older arguments concerning 'free will' and 'determinism'. It
came down very heavily on one side, the side of determinism: human
beings and their consciousness, subjectivity, were totally determined
by social and ideological structures. They were 'made' by history and
society; it was a 'humanist' delusion to think they did any making of
their own. Their 'subjectivity' was not in any sense a free, choosing
consciousness, but was fully 'subject' to dominant ideologies that
were 'inscribed', written into, their consciousness. Only the Althusserians themselves, because they possessed conscious scientific knowledge, escaped this bound condition, these iron determinations.

This kind of marxism used a language all its own, a language not
easily accessible to most people, including most women in the
women's movement. It was a form of marxism generally distanced
from political activity, including feminist political activity, and
resided principally in the universities and colleges. It was seen by
non-adherents as a theoreticist, impenetrable, and narrow doctrine.
Looking back now, the legacy of Althusserian marxism for radical
intellectual life in general has been a widespread rejection of
marxism altogether. Those who now identify marxism as rigid and
mechanistic are often ex-Althusserians who know no other way of
thinking about marxist theory.

Althusserian marxism was very influential in the School of
Humanities and Social Sciences at NSWIT from about 1977 to
around 1983, though there was always a variety of competing views. I
was never an Althusserian marxist. My interest in marxism was far
less rigorous and of a different kind, generally deriving from the use
of it made by British historians, concentrating on its value for
understanding the significance of class and consciousness as explanatory concepts for social and political history. The Marx I liked was
the Marx who wrote the accounts of the mid-nineteenth-century
upheavals in French politics, deploying with flexibility and dexterity
the concepts of state, class, fractions of classes, political mobilisation,

class consciousness, and so on. Yet this kind of marxism was in eclipse in the radical intellectual circles of the late 1970s and early 1980s.

In socialist feminist circles it was Althusserian marxism which was now dominant. Key texts from Britain were: Annette Kuhn and AnnMarie Wolpe (eds) Feminism and Materialism *(1978); Michelle Barrett* Women's Oppression Today: Problems in Marxist Feminist Analysis *(1980), and the British journals* Capital and Class *and, for a time,* Feminist Review. *When Althusserian marxist modes of analysis were focused onto feminist questions, there was, not surprisingly, a definite effect on the character of the questions. The problem posed was no longer 'why are women oppressed?', or more specifically 'why are women oppressed within capitalism?' but 'how is women's oppression* functional *to capitalism?' This body of thought tried to develop feminist versions of current debates in marxist circles about a variety of conceptual issues: the nature of the state, the value of labour power, the functional role of the family for capitalism. In looking over my files, I find a quite substantial body of material I wrote in the late 1970s. Although I was not an Althusserian marxist I was nevertheless influenced by the formulations it was producing. I was drawn onto its theoretical territory—its 'terrain' as its adherents would characteristically have said. In relation to the sexual division of labour, I particularly tried to enter the debate, later referred to as 'the domestic labour debate', on the value to the capitalist economy of women's labour as housewives and mothers. I also got involved with attempts to explain wage discrimination by sex as functional to capitalism, following in particular several articles by Veronica Beechey in British marxist and feminist journals.*

After wrestling with all this for some considerable time I concluded that this body of theory was not useful for trying to explain the sexual division of labour. I set out to develop an alternative account, resting less on those aspects of marxist thought depending on the labour theory of value and more on those aspects resting on the concept of class. Influenced somewhat by Maxine Molyneux's article 'Beyond the Domestic Labour Debate' in the British journal New Left Review *in 1979, I wrote a very short essay for* Refractory Girl, *and revised it for an edited collection of Australian feminist essays in 1980.[1] The original article was in part an appraisal of Molyneux's article; I've left that element of it out in this republication.*

1979–80

Within the family, the man's contribution to childcare and other unpaid domestic work is seen as secondary to his primary task of earning income, while for the woman it is the other way around. Men do not expect, and are not expected to seek, less than a full-time job in order to have time to undertake domestic labour. They may, to some extent, carry out such labour, but only at a level possible outside the working hours of a full-time job; even when unemployed, or when they are sole parents, men's unpaid childcaring will rarely rise above this level. In practice, men are felt to have minimal obligations in daily childcare.

By contrast, women, because of the deeply embedded notion that they are more naturally suited to childcaring—being the biological childbearers—will expect and be expected to undertake a large proportion of this unpaid domestic work. Most women will still expect and be expected to spend some period in their lives as full-time unpaid domestic workers, entirely dependent on their husband's income. Even if the woman participates in the workforce, on either a full-time or a part-time basis, she will still generally expect and be expected to do a considerable proportion of the necessary childcaring and other domestic work outside 'working hours'.

The idea that women are more fitted than men for childcaring and other unpaid domestic work has important results for the experience of each in the workforce. Most significantly, it means that women, having long-term domestic responsibilities and expectations that men do not, will be more likely to enter the workforce on a short-term, intermittent, or part-time basis. Within the working-class family, the woman's income from paid work, although it may be valuable and very often necessary, cannot be continuously relied on. The man's income must be the staple income. Thus the man's income-earning capacity and job security will usually be more important to the family as a whole than will be the woman's. It is more important, therefore, for the male than the female worker to acquire and protect skills, and to organise for increased pay and better working conditions.

Thus the class struggle over men's skills, wage levels, job security and so forth will necessarily be sharper than that over women's job security, status, and pay. In practice, this often means protecting men's jobs from incursions by women, who, being cheaper, will undermine the wage levels obtainable from these jobs. The desire of male workers to exclude women from 'male occupations' is, therefore, not to be dismissed simply as the result of male sexism; it is a logical consequence of the man's greater likelihood of having to support dependants, itself ultimately a consequence of the ideology of motherhood which both men and women share. Only by protecting such occupations can the working class attempt to guarantee a male's job security and wage levels; only by women being restricted to less preferred occupations can the working class as a whole expect to find employment for women which supplements, rather than undermines, the position of the male worker.

Once all this is clear it becomes easier to explain the sexual segregation of occupations and the sexual segmentation of the labour market. This segregation is founded on the fact that men will generally require and fight for higher wages and better jobs than women will. Capital can use this deeply divided workforce in different ways. It can divert men into the more skilled jobs and women into the less skilled. It can maintain whole industries—such as the clothing industry—on the basis of a workforce that will not be demanding a family wage. A differentiated workforce can permit the uneven development of capital and uneven rates of exploitation.

Very often the sexual segregation of occupations is explained in terms of women being confined to occupations which are an extension of the female domestic role into the workplace—nursing, teaching, waitressing, food processing, and so on. But this does not really explain why the sexual segregation of occupations exists and is perpetuated; at best it explains which occupations—given they are to be sexually segregated—women will enter. Even on this level, though, such an explanation is inadequate, for many of the jobs women enter—such as factory process work and clerical work— cannot be particularly characterised as extensions of the female domestic role.

It is the differential wage demand by women and men which lies at the heart of the existence of the sexual segregation of occupations; the question of which will be the male and which will be the female jobs depends on a host of historical determinations. The use of women in jobs closely tied to the female domestic role is only one of these; others include the relative availability of male and female labour at the time of the growth of the occupation; the degree to which the job can be operated, in a way advantageous to capital, on a part-time or casual basis; the degree to which the job requires skill, low labour turnover, and career progression, and so on.

Of course, the workforce is not differentiated solely on a sexual basis—divisions by region, age, ethnic group, and so on may be of at least equal importance, and the argument I am presenting here could also be applied, with modifications, to these divisions.

All this reinforces the sexual division of labour within the family. Whatever views the family members may hold about the naturalness of childcarers being women—that is, whatever the situation ideologically—it will still be logical in the average working-class family for the man to be the primary breadwinner and the woman to be the childcarer on either a full-time or a part-time basis. Quite simply, the man can earn more, and earn more securely, so it is absurd for families to forgo his wage in order that he undertake unpaid childcaring. It is only in situations where the woman's earning power is far above the female average, or where the man's earning power is so great that his part-time income, combined with the woman's full- or part-time income, would be sufficient to support the family, that a couple could realistically contemplate willingly forgoing a part or all of the male wage in this way. Such situations occur in a very small proportion of families overall, and scarcely ever in working-class families. Further, the concentration of women in part-time, casual, or intermittent paid work is not simply a matter of family choice; it is frequently the only kind of work available for women. So again, the allocation to women of most unpaid domestic tasks, including childcaring, becomes a logical as well as an ideological decision.

There is in this way, then, a material basis for the perpetuation of the sexual division of labour in the family and of the ideology of motherhood. The working-class family cannot easily escape this material basis, with the result that ideas about men spending all or part of their 'working' time as childcarers appear unreal and foolish.

It becomes clear, then, that the ideology of motherhood and the unequal sexual segmentation of the labour market are inextricably intertwined. Neither can be fought in isolation; one cannot be undermined unless the other is also undermined. While capitalism remains in economic crisis, and unemployment remains high, the pressure is on to perpetuate and even increase, rather than reduce, this sexual division, especially through the increasing confinement of women to part-time and deskilled work. So any attack on the sexual division of labour in the workforce must be made in the context of a broader strategy aimed at a restructuring of the system of production generally, so that full employment, a shorter working week, and a less hierarchically differentiated job structure can be permanently achieved.

PART IV

Feminism reconsidered

10

Radical feminism

With the publication of 'Explaining the sexual division of labour' I not only broke free of any sense that I needed to work within the problematic of Althusserian marxism. I also regained confidence in my own perspectives on women and work, so much so that I set out to write a book on the history of women and work in Australia since 1945. I could in this way tackle the theoretical problem of explanation on a more solid empirical base.

Yet within a year or two the issues at stake had changed. I was becoming increasingly critical of feminism itself, especially radical feminism but also much that called itself socialist feminism. I did not like the directions feminism seemed to be taking. A turning point came in 1981, when the American theological feminist, Mary Daly, visited Sydney. I was shocked to realise how many of my feminist friends thought this apolitical manhater to be worthwhile, to be a thinker whom they considered they could align themselves with. On reading her Gyn/Ecology, *I found it to be devoid of any socialist perspective, and the epitome of the kind of feminism I did not want to pursue. I was not by any means Daly's only critic in Sydney; she encountered sharp questions at her lecture in Sydney (which I did not attend), and several critiques of her work were written, including notably one by Meaghan Morris.[1] Even so, the episode had revealed to me just how much I had diverged from my closest feminist academic colleagues, and I found it increasingly difficult to find a feminist group which reflected my own particular brand of feminism. I dropped out of the editorial collective which ran* Refractory Girl. *I continued to pursue feminist issues within the workplace, but not outside it other than through my own writing. The following brief account, written for an international collection of feminist and antifeminist writings edited by Robyn Rowland, titled* Women Who Do and Women Who Don't Join the Women's Movement, *outlines this*

process of partial disenchantment, and the thinking that lay behind
it. My work for the next few years was to be really an elaboration of
the points made in this brief essay.

1982

Born in Sydney at the end of the Second World War, I was a 'red
diaper' baby. My parents are both Australians of British descent,
and were members of the Australian Communist Party, which was
then at the height of its influence in Australia. My mother was
actively concerned with 'women's equality', especially in the Union
of Australian Women, within a communist framework of theory
and activity. My father was an Australian communist academic.
During my student days at the University of Sydney I was actively
involved in left-wing politics: in the Campaign for Nuclear Dis-
armament and the Labour Club, later in movements opposing
racist policies and practices towards Australian Aborigines, and
Australia's involvement in the Vietnam War. In relation to the
feminism that was to come later, key influences then were not only
from my mother but also from my reading of the works of Betty
Friedan and Simone de Beauvoir. But I never discussed this reading
with anyone, and indeed regarded 'women's issues' as, in political
terms, trivial, boring and somewhat embarrassing.

It was while I was studying for my doctorate on racism in
Australian history that I first encountered women's liberation. In
December 1969, while marching in a Vietnam War protest demonstration in Sydney, I was confronted by women giving out leaflets
urging women to join a recently formed women's liberation group.
How trivial and diversionary, I thought, in a march opposing a
wholesale destruction of the Vietnamese people. Yet a month later,
when I learnt of a women's liberation meeting to be held at a Left
meeting place, I went. Several women spoke about the need to see
sexual oppression as a real and living force affecting all of us. One
woman spoke about how we as women sought the approval of men,
and devalued each other. This made a great impression on me, for
I recognised it as true of myself. Something, as other feminist
accounts of this sort of experience have put it, had 'clicked'.

I regularly attended women's liberation meetings in Sydney, and
gradually, from discussion and reading of the mainly American
literature, absorbed the feminist perspective: women are oppressed
as women, are given the worst jobs, are economically dependent on
men, are denied abortions, are sexually objectified and generally

devalued. For many of us there, our experiences with New Left men, surely the most aggressively sexist breed alive, made our commitment to women's liberation deep and strong. Sisterhood must be powerful, or we must remain individual victims of sexist ideology. In 1971 I became involved in the production of Sydney's first women's liberation newspaper *Mejane,* and married, my concession to women's liberation being that I did not change my name.

Around 1973–74 the term 'women's liberation' was gradually dropped, and replaced by 'feminism' and the 'women's movement'. I was never too pleased by this, for 'feminism' seemed devoid of socialist politics, while 'women's liberation' referred to a whole set of socialist perspectives. But in time I adopted the new terms and called myself a feminist.

Through the mid-1970s I was involved in having a baby, finishing my doctoral thesis, and then acting as a co-ordinator for two years of the women's studies courses at the Australian National University in Canberra. My intellectual concerns were increasingly with the study of women and work. I returned to Sydney, to take up my present position as a lecturer, and to be involved in the editing of a feminist journal, *Refractory Girl* (the title taken from an early nineteenth-century Australian convict women's song).

What, then, do I think feminism is about? Feminism is not one single ideology or movement. The varieties of feminism are held together only by a common commitment to seeking some kind of better life for women as women. For me, feminism is about both a political and a personal assertion of the ideal of sexual equality, and about working for the achievement of that ideal. But not all feminists would accept this notion, many rejecting any ideal of equality or any hope of a sexually egalitarian world. For such feminists, men are the enemy, and the task of feminism is rather one of creating women-identified women, of 'getting men out of our heads'. Even within those strands of feminism that do subscribe to the ideal of sexual equality, there are differences between those who concentrate on immediate political and industrial changes, those who focus on achieving psychological and ideological change, and those who ally the struggle for sexual equality with the struggle for socialism.

The chief values of feminism for me are these. First, it provides a means of gaining insight into those psychological processes embedded in family experiences and sexist ideology generally, whereby we are all constructed as 'masculine' or 'feminine', and are psychologically limited (and if female, guilt-ridden and dependent) as a result. Second, my brand of feminism denies the basically biologically determinist argument that women's childbearing functions necessarily determine for them a confinement of tasks to childcaring and housework. It argues that childcaring, and indeed all other human activities, should be shared between men and women. Third, feminism points to the institutional bulwarks of sexual inequality—in the family, in the workplace, in cultural life, and in politics. Feminism argues that apparent choices are institutionally framed. For these reasons, I must continue to call myself a feminist. But I am increasingly critical of some of the directions recent feminism seems to be taking. I have begun to think that many feminists *are* anti-male in a crude sense, *are* simply seeking their own advancement *vis-à-vis* middle-class men, *have* abandoned socialist ideals and organisations, and *are* out of touch with or unsympathetic to the very real problems of working-class people, both female and male. Living with two males and no females as I do, I find discussions in some feminist groups about whether men are 'the enemy' utterly absurd. Not having rejected men at a personal, emotional and sexual level, I find those developments within feminist theory which depend on such a rejection uncongenial. I find many recent feminist characterisations of men to be bordering on the racist, to be, in fact, a reversion to the biological determinism we once so fiercely rejected.

This return to biological determinism leads to a rejection of the ideal of men and women sharing childcaring, on the grounds that men are evil incarnate, and children should therefore be reared by women only. In some versions it leads to a moral prescription against having children at all. The earlier interest in the processes of the construction of people as 'masculine' and 'feminine' comes to be replaced by a position which sees men as the all-powerful definers of patriarchy, and *women* as the socially constructed, the other. Women's task thus becomes one of recovering their 'stolen energies' from the all-powerful, the one—men. 'Patriarchy' becomes an all-embracing term, and with its use, or over-use, comes the abandonment of the task of *explanation* of sexual inequality and difference altogether.

Feminism is now under renewed attack from the forces of the Right, the new moral conservatism. These forces combine a highly individualistic and extreme *laissez faire* ideology in relation to the state, with a defence of the patriarchal (in the old power-of-the-father sense) family, of female economic dependence, of female-only privatised childcaring, sexist ideology generally, and specifically a denial of the right to full reproductive control. Their ascendancy reminds us that the recent gains have been hard-won, and are easily lost.

In this context one becomes wary of being too critical of current feminist theory and practice. But it's all the more important in this new embattled context for feminists to reappraise their own priorities, ideology, and strategies. There are two key issues here: first, the question of socialism and the relation of feminism to it; second, the question of the family, childcare, and children.

Feminists need to recognise more than many of them do that their concerns are not the only concerns of great importance. Also important are: the increasing possibility of nuclear war, the destructiveness and gross inequality produced by capitalism, the reassertion and strengthening of a truly socialist movement, and the ending of racism (especially in Australia as it affects Aborigines). Recognition must enable feminists to see that some women can be underprivileged *as women* but very privileged indeed if they are well-off financially, politically powerful, or if they do not belong to a dispossessed minority. The notion of 'women's oppression' tends to obscure the reality of those cases of female privilege and male underprivilege arising from class or ethnic group.

Yet if feminism, through its notion of 'women's oppression', tends to obscure a class analysis and a socialist politics, there are two ways in which its political effects are more positive. One is that many middle-class women, through their active involvement in feminism, have been brought face to face with the harsh realities of many working-class women's lives, with the effects of living in a society where childcaring renders women economically dependent on men whose own wages are low and insecure, where material poverty lays the basis for tense and violent family situations.

The other way in which feminism affects class relationships in a positive way lies in its influence on some working-class women, especially those active or becoming active in their trade unions or in other kinds of workplace action. Feminist demands for abortion, childcare, and equal pay have a lot of support amongst working-class women, but what does not have their support, on the whole, is the feminist rejection of the family, and its apparent rejection of mothering.

Feminists often attack 'the family' while anti-feminists claim to defend it. In my view this is a simplistic division, for one can be a feminist and yet defend the family as a residential and emotional unit, or an anti-feminist and advocate policies which undermine it. It's about time feminists began sweeping the ground from under the feet of the Right, not by defending 'the family' per se, but by defending those values which it is held to represent: long-term relationships, emotional commitment, kinship ties, and especially the importance of the close bonding which occurs between parents and children. We need to sever the connection so many feminists assume between, on the one hand, a critique of the present structure of the family, with its economic dependence for women, association of daily childcare with women rather than with men and women equally, its psycho-pathology and privatisation, and, on the other, a rejection of family life altogether, of the co-residence and emotional ties between parents and their children.

We need to say more strongly than we have that having children should be a positive experience, and even under present conditions has strong positive elements. While feminism has successfully and rightly attacked the ideology that women should and must have children, and has eloquently defended women's right to make other choices, it needs also to assert equally successfully the right of all women to have children without the financial stress, economic dependence, double burden or confinement to childcaring only which children in this society so often entail.

This means taking seriously the deep needs in adults that children satisfy, the rights of children as individuals, and the importance of developing residential and work patterns that take both of these considerations fully into account. It means advocating policies and practices which ensure for children stable home environments, links with the world beyond the home via childcare centres and schooling and community activities, parents who have links with the world outside the home, and equal responsibility taken by men and women. It means insisting that such things will never be available to all children equally as long as we have an exploitative, inegalitarian capitalist system. And it means a reevaluation of feminism's emphasis on individual self-expression and independence, and a facing of the fact that on the other side of the equation are those key concerns of security, commitment, and continuity. We just have to get the balance right.

In the long run being female *does* matter, trying to write a gender-conscious class analysis of Australian society *does* seem worth doing. And I'll keep writing, for all those thirteen years' experience are still there, the issues do matter. But next time I don't think I'll see myself as part of an oppressed group, and I won't submerge those larger issues of war, exploitation, and poverty. I see the choices facing me now not as arising only from my being female, but also from my being relatively privileged in a crazy and inegalitarian world.

11

The problem with 'patriarchy'

I began to develop the critique of the concepts of patriarchy and 'women's oppression' which I had begun in 'Radical Feminism'. I was, in the course of this critique, beginning to defend marxism as useful for talking about women just as it was going out of fashion in radical intellectual circles. Perhaps I am just contrary. While marxism was in the ascendant in the late 1970s I was not part of it and wrote nothing on women in that tradition. Once it went on the decline from the early 1980s, convicted of providing a simplified and totalising view of society, I began to defend it more openly. But marxism for me and the Althusserians were two quite different things.

As part of this critique, I reviewed in 1982 (I think) for the educational radio station in Sydney, 2SER, an American book edited by Lydia Sargeant, called Women and Revolution *(1981).*

1982

Lydia Sargeant's book, *Women and Revolution: A Discussion of the Unhappy Marriage of Marxism and Feminism*, is currently being widely discussed in the women's movement. It is not as much about problems, actions, or strategy as its name might imply; it is rather about how we should explain the social distinction between men and women. The implication of the collection is that it will be easier to develop a strategy for revolutionising the relations between the sexes once we have a clear analysis of why existing relations take the form they do.

The key chapter is by American Heidi Hartmann, called 'The Unhappy Marriage of Marxism and Feminism: Towards a More Progressive Union'. It first appeared as a journal article in 1979. Hartmann argues that the various attempts to develop a theory of women's position which combine the insights of both marxism and feminism have failed. They have failed because in the supposed synthesis of marxism and feminism which produces socialist feminist theory, marxism is dominant. Marxism, which is useful for understanding the workings of capitalism in general, is useless, says Hartmann, for explaining issues to do with sex and gender:

> While Marxist analysis provides essential insight into the laws of historical development, and those of capital in particular, the categories of marxism are sex-blind. Only a specifically feminist analysis reveals the systemic character of relations between men and women ... The categories of marxist analysis, class, reserve army of labour, wage-labourer, do not explain why particular people fill particular places.

It is the concept of patriarchy, Hartmann argues, which enables us to do this: 'Gender and racial hierarchies determine who fills the empty places ... It is in studying patriarchy that we learn why it is women who are dominated and how.'

She concludes that women now face two separate forms of oppression—the one deriving from capitalism, which creates a form of oppression women share with men, the other deriving from patriarchy, the institutionalised control of women by men. Any analysis of women's oppression must recognise both capitalism and patriarchy as important, seeing them as separate, though in practice related, social structures. A dual mode of apprehending the world must be accepted, so that one stops trying to develop marxist interpretations of the issues thrown up by radical feminism.

Hartmann's argument has been found so compelling by American socialist feminists that it has been made the centrepiece of this book. Thirteen contributions have been collected to discuss Hartmann's argument, most of them supporting her case. The main line of argument of the opponents is that we don't want two theories to explain women's position—one marxist and the other feminist—but rather one theory, a revitalised feminist marxism. Hartmann returns at the end of the book to say she is not convinced by those who argue for a single rather than a dual theory for explaining social life. It is possible, she says, to be a feminist who supports capitalism or a socialist who opposes sexual equality. There are two separate perspectives involved, though many might wish to have them both.

This is a frustrating book. Most of the contributors have a

peculiar notion of what marxism is. They see it essentially as a theory of economics, rather than a theory of the ways economic matters relate to political, social, and cultural ones. Furthermore, all of them accept the idea of patriarchy as a separate social structure.

The initial insights of the women's liberation movement have become rigidified, so that concepts like patriarchy are no longer open, but rather close off avenues of inquiry. 'Patriarchy' has become a troublesome concept for feminist theory. Using the term to refer to male power and control makes it difficult to adhere to the older, and I think more precise and helpful usage where 'patriarchy' refers to 'the rule of the father'. Another and fundamental problem is that patriarchy as it is now used has become a misleading concept: it explains nothing; it helps us to change nothing. It presumes the answers to the questions we ask. We need in particular to reconsider the idea of 'male dominance' or 'male supremacy' which the concept of patriarchy is meant to explain. That is, while there are many inequalities between men and women, and many ways in which men can control or exert power over women, I don't think that one can encapsulate all this as 'male supremacy'. Such a view treats all men as a group and all women as a group, and then says that all men have power over all women. I think it's all more complicated than that. Other power relationships and inequalities cut across sexual ones.

12

Politics and sisterhood

Later that year I left Australia, on academic study leave, for six months. I attended an international conference on women's studies in Montreal, and then spent several months in London. At neither the conference nor in London did I manage to find anyone with quite the same position as mine. Everyone seemed either too close to the forms of feminism I had been criticising, or else not interested in feminist questions and issues at all. While in London I wrote the following report of the Montreal conference. It gave me the opportunity to pursue the problem of the relationship between marxism and feminism a little further.

This essay was printed in Arena *no. 62 in 1983. In this republication I have departed from my rule of not meddling with the original, as, on rereading, the original essay struck me as cryptic indeed. So this version is longer than that which appeared in* Arena.

1982

For marxists and socialists, the area known as women's studies is problematic. On the one hand, it can so very easily depend on radical feminist notions of 'women's oppression' and 'patriarchy' which in fact run counter to marxist analyses. On the other, it continually generates and develops discussion of some of the most important issues in socialist and marxist debate.

This difficulty posed by women's studies is a specific instance of the more general problems modern feminism poses for socialists and marxists. On the positive side, feminism has served to revitalise

that old (nineteenth-century) socialist concern with issues surrounding the institutions of marriage and 'the family', and sexuality
and reproductive control. It has provided women within the labour
movement with a language in which to challenge unthinking (and
thinking) sexist attitudes and practices in that movement. It has
drawn a large number of middle-class women into the sphere of
radical alternative politics, and has thereby facilitated some reordering of gender relations within the middle class. Feminism has
strengthened the pressure for certain state policies benefiting the
working class (greater availability of abortion, emergency refuges
and rape crisis centres, lone-parent benefits, childcare provisions,
etc.) And it has encouraged a rethinking and a new activism around
a whole range of concerns: women's wages, trade union organisation and practice, the 'social wage', the construction of culture and
ideology.

On the negative side, feminism has been part of a more general
process whereby class-based understandings and perspectives have
been undermined. The proposition put forward by feminism—that
women as a group are oppressed by men as a group, or by the social
system—brings feminism into direct conflict with marxism.
Whereas the task of a marxist class analysis is to assert common
class interests, culture, and structural situation across gender and
other ascriptive lines, the task of feminism is to assert a unity
between women. The incompatibility between the two forms of
analysis is most evident when characterising the structural position
of working-class men: feminism sees them as oppressors, while a
class analysis sees them as exploited and oppressed. Kate Millett
saw clearly the possible complications a class analysis might pose
for feminist theory, and explicitly rejected the salience of class: 'In a
society where status is dependent upon the economic, social, and
educational circumstances of class, it is possible for certain females
to appear to stand higher than some males. Yet not when one looks
more closely at the subject ...'[1]

The notion of 'women's oppression' provides immediate problems for class analysis of society. It relies on the view that 'women'
and 'men' are meaningful social groups which can be said to have
this or that character and situation. This character is often given a
biological base, but even where biological determinism is emphati-
cally rejected, feminists still make huge generalisations about what
'men' and 'women' are like, and what they experience.

Yet 'men' and 'women' are not simple, unproblematic, self-
evident totalities of concrete individuals, but are rather historically
and variably constructed categories. While the ascriptions 'male'
and 'female' have deep social meaning, it does not follow that either
women or men constitute meaningful social groups. They may be so
constituted, for example in societies where there are few other

sources of social division and difference. But in societies divided by class, ethnic group, race, or nationality, neither men nor women will form a single social group. Political movements and cultural practices may work to reinforce identity as male and female, to mobilise men and women as self-conscious groups. But in our kind of society these movements and practices cannot really succeed in any sustained way, for always the category of people which is potentially able to be called into being as a self-conscious social group is being constantly split apart by class and ethnic allegiances.

Feminists who follow the ideas of Michel Foucault are adept at pointing out the multiplicity of ways in which the categories 'men' and 'women' are constructed and given meaning, but it is rarely emphasised that feminism itself is one of the forces constructing these categories. Indeed the use of the categories 'men' and 'women' in this way by many feminists is not altogether dissimilar to the way conventional sexist ideology constructs them. Conventional sexism asserts that men and women are distinct social groups with certain distinct and different qualities (capacities, needs, desires), rights, and duties. Conservatives will say: It is for women to bear and nurture children; it is for men to provide for and defend kith and kin. Their defence of the family, and attack on feminism, is couched in terms of what 'men' and 'women' as distinct social groups are, experience, and should be.

Feminism also makes statements about what men and women are, experience, and should be. In particular feminists typically argue that all women everywhere and at all times lack power and privilege, which is confined to men. Any apparent exceptions (very wealthy women, political leaders, top businesswomen) are written off as illusions, in that their wealth or power is derived only from their relationship to a particular man, or as meaningless aberrations serving to mask the fact that most people who hold such power are male. In both cases, the feminist and the sexist, the possibility that gender divisions can at time be overridden, or suppressed, by other forms of division, is not seriously entertained.

Some writers attempt to go only halfway along the line of argument I am advancing here. Thus English feminist Jenny Somerville wishes to attack the concept of 'patriarchy' yet retain that of 'women's oppression'.[2] She sees the problem with 'patriarchy' as resting in its attempt to construct a unitary principle of explanation for women's oppression; and the feminist desire for a unitary principle of analysis of sexual division as being as objectionable as the 'dogmatism of marxist theory'. We should rather, she says, insist on the specificity, the multiple forms, of that oppression. But the notion of 'women's oppression' is as suspect as that of 'patriarchy', for it depends on a unitary concept of women and relies on a particularly unclear and analytically unusable concept:

'oppression'. 'Exploitation' can be given a precise meaning, located in a particular notion of capitalism; 'oppression' cannot.

Marxist critiques of aspects of feminist theory can add to those of Somerville, and others in the British journal *m/f*. This is not to argue that marxism as it now exists is adequate to coming to terms with gender and sexual division; rather it is to say that any analysis we can develop should be seen in terms of extending the present boundaries of marxist approaches. Concepts such as 'women's oppression' and 'patriarchy' do not in fact extend those boundaries; they run counter to the whole enterprise. This incompatibility is being recognised, especially by those who have struggled most valiantly to combine the two. Some, like Heidi Hartmann, argue that we will have to rest content with a dualistic mode of analysis: feminism for patriarchy, marxism for capitalism.[3]

It seems to me possible, however, to pursue another path, the attempt to develop a marxist approach to understanding those phenomena to which feminism has so importantly drawn our attention: the family–workforce relationship, sexist ideology, domestic violence and rape, divisions of labour based on gender, and so on. It is not necessary or useful for those engaged in the study of women to jettison marxist theory, in particular the notion of class. 'Class' is not only a means for conceptually delineating differences between women, or between men, but is a framework within which sexual division is itself elaborated, formed, constituted. So, too, is class formed within the framework of sexual division. Understanding sexual division and understanding class are, therefore, not two separate processes. That is, a reassertion of the fundamental importance of class relationships does not mean a jettisoning of key feminist concerns, but rather a recasting of the way we approach them. On drawing back from the central feminist propositions of 'women's oppression' and 'patriarchy' our conceptions of capitalism and socialism are now nevertheless irrevocably influenced by feminist critiques, and by the feminist revitalisation of a recognition of the importance of gender generally. Whatever the fundamental differences in analytical standpoints, socialists and marxists cannot divorce themselves from the remarkable energies and insights thrown up by the feminist ferment.

Women's studies developed as the academic wing of the modern feminist movement. As such it is based on a feminist conception of women as a meaningful social category. Yet it has room, too, for all kinds of approaches to the problem of gender and sexual division, and marxists have made their mark on the field, especially in analyses of the relationship between familial/household structures and the operations of the social and detailed divisions of labour within capitalist production.

It was with these contradictory feelings about women's studies, and marxism and feminism, that I recently attended the First International Conference on Research and Teaching Related to Women, in Montreal from 26 July to 4 August, 1982. Organised by the Simone de Beauvoir Institute at Concordia University, Montreal, it was attended by over 300 women (and a handful of men) from over 80 countries. The conference did little to indicate to me the way forward, or the latest developments within women's studies. It was interesting, nevertheless, in providing a picture of the very different institutional frameworks within which women's studies is undertaken internationally. If the marxists were in a minority, there were enough there (mainly from South America, and some from Algeria and the Middle East) to make some telling points about the internal contradictions within women's studies in particular, and feminism generally. And there were some important points made, not only by marxists, on the whole question of the place of intellectuals, of teachers and researchers generally, in relation to the people they teach and study.

The conference was a strange amalgam of UN-based interests in incorporating women into Third World economic and social 'development', and radical feminist traditions of scholarship. This followed from its origins. The conference had initially been suggested at a UNESCO-organised meeting in Paris in May 1980, and then more strongly at the women's studies seminars held in the context of the UN World Conference on Women, in Copenhagen in July 1980. The purpose of the conference, as outlined by the organisers, was to discuss, internationally, the problems facing women's studies, and to strengthen international communication between its practitioners. This in fact meant, by and large, talking *about* women's studies rather than actually exchanging views on some of the substantive issues raised within it. The few exceptions to this (for example, papers on women and work, on the historical origins of the modern position of different groups of Arab women, and others on the work of Simone de Beauvoir) were welcome indeed but did not, most unfortunately, form the core of the conference.

The organisers stressed the need to keep the conference small and geographically representative. While the desire for real international exchange was laudable, this meant in effect a large degree of separation of the conference from the Canadian women's studies world. For example, the very interesting group of Canadians, some of them marxists, who had earlier attended the Women and Labour Conference in Adelaide, were not present, and many other leading Canadian workers in the field were also not involved.

The people who came to the conference were mainly academics, teaching undergraduate and graduate courses on women. Others were directors and other workers at special research centres within academic institutions devoted to studying women. Many of the

Third World women appeared to me to be near-government spokes-people, though others were highly critical of their governments. Like one of the Algerian women who spoke in the final session, I was amazed to see the breadth of institutionalised feminism, the numbers of women present who spoke as government officials, or, more often, as consultants to those officials.

Most of the main points to be discussed throughout the con-ference were raised in the first plenary session. But it was hard to see this at the time: through the haze of language difficulties, imperfect simultaneous translation, malfunctioning translation equipment, and widely divergent assumptions by speakers about the nature of their audience, much of the debate in the early stages was quite opaque. But a rereading of the printed papers makes it clear that what was being argued was, in brief: academic research on women must be tied to the needs of the local and international women's movement; must operate in a situation where the people being studied work with the researchers on an equal basis so that the 'experts' become simply technicians at the service of the people; must be feminist in starting from an assumption that women are op-pressed by men and male-dominated institutions; must necessarily take greater account of qualitative and 'subjective' issues than do other (male-dominated) kinds of study, and is itself a kind of scientific revolution in overthrowing the assumption embedded in all other scientific discourse of the correspondence that human equals masculine. There was strong disagreement over whether women's studies had a logic, epistemological basis, and method-ology all its own. Many speakers did seem to believe that women's studies necessarily has an anti-logical-positivist position which is peculiar to it. These issues were not argued out very clearly, and the disagreements here continued throughout the conference.

A second strand running throughout was a concern with the connection between women's studies and social change. Most discussion of this was over two issues: (1) how to influence governments more effectively, and (2) how to put one's research at the service of the women being studied. The fact that these two con-cerns were often totally contradictory was not very well dealt with. In the session on 'Research and Social Action', where both issues arose constantly, one Brazilian speaker angrily pointed out that the discussion was ignoring the fact that in Third World countries it was nearly always ruling-class women who had access to research at all, and *they* wouldn't change much. The term 'social action' was obscuring the issue of which side you were on in class and political terms. Feminists, she insisted, simply could not piously wish away class conflict and state power.

The difficulties facing committed feminist research were often perceived mainly in terms of feminists' (or, more generally, women's) difficulty in getting access to government or private funding, though some North American speakers didn't seem to think the difficulty was very great ('You can get conservative funding for radical research', said one). Despite what the Brazilian speaker said, most continued to talk as if we were all agreed on what we wanted to achieve through our research. Peggy McIntosh, from the Center for Research on Women, Wellesley College, Massachussetts, spoke of one study undertaken at the centre which was of women and management in the private sector, funded by a private corporation. The research concluded that there were various barriers to women's progression through the corporate hierarchy and that this lowered productivity. The implication was that the corporation reacted by removing these barriers, and, presumably, increased productivity. This analysis was made without any recognition that other women there might oppose private industry, or working in management, altogether.

Many of the speakers, and the organisers, attempted to portray differences merely as variations based on different national and historical experiences. Conflict was held to be impossible between women, who were seen as an essentially indivisible group. In the end, this notion was challenged not so much through the formal papers and discussions, as through the irruption of current political conflicts into the conference agenda.

Israel was bombing Beirut at the time, and indeed the conference itself was very directly affected by this issue, not only by the presence of Lebanese, Palestinian, and Israeli women but also by the fact that the main Lebanese speaker, Julinda Abu Nasr, was unable to attend. It became palpably clear that the version of feminism dominant at the conference had no way of dealing with such issues. The first attempt to move a motion opposing Israel's bombing of Beirut and supporting the Palestinian cause was ruled out of order, though a speaker from the Union of Palestinian Women was received warmly when she spoke against the Israeli invasion of Lebanon. When a second attempt was made to move a resolution noting the absence of the Lebanese delegate and opposing Israeli policies towards the Palestinian people, the response of the organisers was to stifle discussion and to relegate it to an extra session in a separate room.

Early in the conference a Haitian woman (not a conference delegate) from Montreal, where there is a large Haitian immigrant population, attempted to speak. She was asked to wait, and then when she did attempt to speak later, the chairperson closed the meeting and the interpreters ceased work. Those of us who could not understand French were then bewildered, as the French-speaking women erupted into a very loud emotional argument, the only English words spoken being, in the middle of it all, 'take your fucking bullshit somewhere else'. Only later, via a multi-lingual leaflet handed out at the door the next day, did I discover what it had all been about. The issue was in fact an important one: the only Haitian delegate was Miss Marie-Carmelle Lafontant, a well-known supporter of the Duvalier regime, and known as a 'fillette Lalo' (a female agent of the repressive Duvalier police). What the woman who had been refused the right to speak had been asking for was a boycott of Miss Lafontant's paper, and conference endorsement of her opposition to the fact that Miss Lafontant, and not a member of the Haitian diaspora as earlier requested, had been invited as the Haitian delegate.

Thus the ideology of an apolitical women's studies conference, stressing sisterhood rather than those political conflicts which found women on opposing sides, had been used to muzzle criticism of the methods of selection of delegates from countries under repressive regimes. But the attacks on this apolitical notion of feminism nevertheless continued, and as the conference wore on, discussion of these issues (but not motion-putting) was of necessity increasingly allowed. The notion of sisterhood had taken yet another beating, though the final result was inconclusive, as it must have been amongst such a politically diverse group.

13

A short history of feminism, 1970–1984

Back in Australia in 1983 I developed my critique of certain aspects of feminist theory in a paper to a conference on 'Women and Social Justice' at ANU in October. In this paper I placed my critique in the context of a history of debates within the women's movement since 1970. The version which follows differs slightly from the paper as given to the conference and subsequently published in a collection entitled Unfinished Business: Women and Social Justice in Australia, *in that some additional argument has been added towards the end, taking the account up to 1984.*[1]

1983–4

Women's Liberation, 1970–72

When feminism suddenly strengthened as a political ideology and a political force in Australia in 1970, it was known as 'Women's Liberation'. This title reflected the new movement's origins in radical 'New Left' politics, itself grounded in the student movement of the late 1960s. The point was that those who had been supporting the liberation of oppressed Third World peoples (as in Vietnam) had forgotten to tidy their own backyard. New Left men who had been so concerned about the fate of the Vietnamese had been embedded in a 1960s sexual permissiveness, happily dominating, denigrating, and exploiting New Left women, and those women had

finally had enough. The early women's liberation movement, while
in part a revolt against New Left men, was nevertheless imbued
with New Left politics. It was concerned with imperialism, socialism, and the oppression of Third World and minority groups, with
the ideologies sustaining an evil capitalist system, with revolutionary strategy and tactics. Organisationally, the new movement took
more from anarchist than socialist traditions, but ideologically, at
first, the socialist tradition was dominant.

One of the earliest pamphlets produced by a women's liberation
group in Australia was called *Only the Chains Have Changed*, and
was printed in Balmain. This pamphlet identified women as an
oppressed group, linking women's oppression with the war in
Vietnam. It was distributed at an anti-Vietnam War march in
December 1969. It concluded: 'We, like the Vietnamese, can only
be free of oppression when the profit makers no longer have the
power to determine our lives.'

The connection of early women's liberation with the New Left
meant that marxists had a lot to contribute to early feminist theory,
explaining women's oppression as a product of capitalism. Three
overseas writers were particularly influential: Juliet Mitchell, Margaret Benston, and Peggy Morton. Mitchell's book *Woman's Estate*
(1971) was based on an earlier article which appeared in *New Left
Review* in 1966.[2] It was Mitchell who showed most clearly that the
new movement presented theoretical and political challenges for
marxism. She said we needed to provide marxist answers to feminist
questions, a view widely rejected in the women's movement today,
even by socialist feminists. She did not really indicate, however,
what these marxist answers might be. In that sense she did not
provide a theoretical basis for the marxist feminism she proposed.

Benston's 'The Political Economy of Women's Liberation'
appeared in Australia in mimeographed form in 1970.[3] Benston (a
Canadian) argued that women are oppressed as a distinct group
because they do unpaid housework and men do not. The survival of
capitalism depended both on the privatisation of housework/child-
care *and* its allocation to women. Only in this way could domestic
labour be done cheaply, women retained as a 'reserve army of
labour', and social stability maintained. Her solution, following
Engels and Lenin, was for the industrial revolution to invade the
household, but with socialist, not capitalist, relations of production.
Another Canadian, Peggy Morton (1970), took up the argument and
suggested that the problem with Benston's view was that it could
not account for the relationship between women's domestic and
paid labour.[4] She also suggested a more precise definition of the
family which is seen as the means by which labour power is
maintained and reproduced. Both Benston and Morton looked for a
material basis for women's oppression under capitalism. Their

formulations were to have far-reaching consequences for later marxist feminist debate.

These views were influential among the early women's liberation groups here. A mimeographed two-page sheet entitled 'Women's Liberation and the Left', printed in January 1970 by the Sydney Women's Liberation Group, was concerned with just these questions. It argued that 'like other leftwing analyses, the ideas of women's liberation link oppression in society with exploitation'. Women were oppressed because their underpaid and marginal wage labour was 'a boon to employers', and their unpaid domestic labour was a boon to all men. Thus from the outset, analyses developing in Sydney were following a path similar to that of Morton and Benston. These analyses were remarkable for their attempt to weld feminist insights to marxist class-based understandings. But they did not constitute a theory explaining *middle-* (as well as working-) class women's oppression which the feminist movement needed. The social base of modern feminism was that expanding group of women who were entering the professional, technical, administrative and skilled occupations. This group, and its male counterpart, was the product of the changing occupational structure, the expansion of the tertiary sector, and of the related extension of education. They occupied a relatively privileged position by virtue of education and recognised skills, and they were becoming increasingly unionised. First as students, this group formed the basis of the New Left and later of feminist, ecological, and other radical movements.

For the middle-class and skilled working-class women who constituted the social base for feminism, 'gender' was a more compelling issue than 'class'. Comparatively, such women tend not to be particularly disadvantaged by class: typically they have access to education, jobs and reasonable levels of pay, or support from a man earning a good salary. But they are disadvantaged by gender. They can see men of their own social class reaching positions involving good incomes and often power; they feel devalued at every level on the basis of their sex; they are subject to sexual exploitation and objectification and sexist ideology, to the fear of rape and so on. The women's liberation movement spoke to this growing group of women. It recognised and explained their problems and proposed modes of action. The new movement quickly attracted to it many women who had no connection with Left or socialist ideals at all.

The key element in early women's liberation argument was that women are oppressed on the basis hen housework, childcare, work determinism. The key issues were housework, childcare, work opportunities, pay, abortion, and sexual exploitation and objectification. Working-class women were usually seen to suffer more than middle-class women from various forms of oppression in all these areas, but the real point was that middle-class women suffered too. Far from being privileged, middle-class women were part of an oppressed group: women. As the argument gathered speed, and took a more distinctly radical feminist turn, women's oppression—including middle-class women's oppression—increasingly became not merely an additional kind of oppression, analogous to if not as serious as the oppression of minority groups and Third World peoples. Women's oppression became the basic kind of oppression, a kind of oppression, in fact, on which all others were built.

Radical feminism, with its emphasis on sexual subjugation rather than class, dovetailed with other Australian political and intellectual developments. The ground had been well laid during the 1960s by many intellectuals who had concluded that Australia was becoming a classless society. This view had its origins in the end-of-ideology thesis of the 1950s and held that as the working class became more affluent, through rising prosperity, it was acquiring many features of the middle class, even becoming middle-class. Those who had failed to make it into the petit bourgeois world were considered not as working class (the proletariat which might endanger the capitalist system which created it), but as special categories—the poor, the migrant, the Aboriginal. Class hatreds, and the old conflict between capital and labour so evident to everyone in the 1930s and 1940s, were now obsolete. Unionised males were redefined as the 'haves' who were, along with employers and governments, oppressing the 'have-nots'. Women's liberation added a new category to the 'have-nots'. Women, as unpaid housewives, poorly paid workers, welfare beneficiaries and single parents, were the really poor. Even Aboriginal and migrant men were occasionally excluded from the ranks of the 'have-nots', for they had their women to oppress and treat as personal slaves.

Many early feminists were aware of the weakness of this analysis. A paper by Barbara Levy, delivered to the first national Women's Liberation conference in Melbourne in 1970, argued that the movement had to broaden its membership to include working-class women, whose 'oppression is much more apparent'. She pointed out that the initial membership of the movement came from the organised Left, and consisted of women who either had or were acquiring a tertiary education, were generally childless, and used to a 'relatively active independent life'. Working-class women's experiences were different, as they continually juggled the difficult alternatives of unpaid childcare and 'process work in a noisy factory'. The possibility for a political unity between these two groups, she thought, lay in the fact that 'the institutions and attitudes that oppress women—the family, femininity, male chauvinism—cut across class lines and qualify class allegiances'. The perspective of this paper became characteristic of women's liberation: an awareness of class differences between women, coupled with an assertion of the unity of their oppression. Women's oppression 'both complements and contradicts a class analysis'. The tasks of the new women's movement included the description of sexism, sexist ideology, sexual inequality. A vast feminist literature emerged detailing sexual inequalities in education, the workplace, political life, the family, and sexist assumptions in cultural areas such as literature, art, children's books, advertising and the media. A second task was to formulate demands. These included equal pay, free 24-hour childcare, work opportunities, the right to abortion. In the early seventies the problem of employment was perceived to be not so much one of availability as the *kind* of jobs open to women. This was in part a plea for wider work opportunities by educated women whose job options were restricted because of sex discrimination.

These perspectives were clearly evident in the early newspaper *Mejane*, produced in Sydney from 1971 to 1974. Its title reflected an assertion of sisterhood, the rejection of male-defined otherness. It published a blend of domestic and overseas news and reviews of overseas books. Early *Mejanes* carried articles by men alongside strongly radical feminist outpourings and confessionals, a combination which is hardly possible today. Its logic was an identification of women as a group, and an identification by middle-class women with working-class women—cleaners, machinists, inmates of girls' homes, prisoners.

But the problem of explanation remained unsolved. It was not enough to describe the manifestations of sexism and sexual inequality or to make demands; we needed an explanation to counter the biologistic approach. This was hard to find. It had to cover not only our society in our time, but also the fact of sexual inequality in all societies at all times. And it could not be grounded in biological difference. Having posited a universal oppression, the explanation for it could not hinge on anything too specific, anything that would be useful for understanding some societies but not others. The early marxist attempts seemed to fail because they attributed women's oppression to capitalism. Women's oppression was much older than capitalism. As American feminist anthropologist Rayna Rapp Reiter put it in 'The Search for Origins: Unravelling the Threads of Gender Hierarchy': 'Whatever we conclude about the effects of capitalism on the status of women, it is clear that the system is built upon forms of sexual hierarchy which have still deeper roots ... there exist more ancient layers of gender differentiation and discrimination.'[5] If women's oppression could not be attributed to capitalism, why then did it exist at all? What were its sources? One strand stressed de Beauvoir's (and before her, Wollstonecraft's and J.S. Mill's) dictum, 'woman is made, not born'. The emphasis here was on 'sex roles', the acquisition of a gendered identity through the processes of socialisation, or 'social conditioning'. This rested on a notion of a neutral body which subsequently, through social assignment as 'male' or 'female', provides the basis for the acquisition of a feminine or masculine identity and social role.[6] Women and men are as they are because they have been taught to be thus. Such an outlook provided a ready reply to biologistic arguments, but by itself it could not come to grips with the question of why such sex roles exist in the first place. It could only explain how sex roles are reproduced.

One radical feminist to address the problem of *why*? was Shulamith Firestone.[7] Like Morton and Benston, she was interested in locating women's oppression in a material base, but for her this base was not capitalism but rather the biological human duality in reproduction. This biological duality she saw as socially institutionalised 'in the interests of men'. If women were to be free, therefore, men must share in human reproduction (childbearing and childcaring) itself. She has often been rejected for her biological determinism, and her test-tube-baby solution, but she was significant for her use of biological difference as *explanation* rather than *justification* for sexual inequality.

But the most profound ideological influence was Kate Millett's *Sexual Politics* (1970), which eschewed Firestone's, Benston's and Morton's search for a material base for women's oppression. Millett redefined 'patriarchy' for the modern feminist movement. She uses the term variously to mean an institution, a governing ideology, a set of institutions (the family, society, and the state), and a kind of society, as in 'our society, like all other historical civilisations, is a patriarchy'.[8] Through all these varying usages, there is a common concern to identify patriarchy as the institutionalised rule of women by men. She is concerned not so much to explain as to describe, not so much with inequality as with sexual domination, hence her title *Sexual Politics*. For Millett, patriarchy is historically, not biologically, created: 'While patriarchy as an institution is a social constant so deeply entrenched as to run through all other political, social, or economic forms, whether of caste or class, feudality or bureaucracy, just as it pervades all major religions, it also exhibits great variety in history and locale'.[9] Despite the stress on patriarchy's historicity, however, Millett pays little attention to examining the reasons for its existence or persistence. In terms of historical and sociological understanding, she is content to argue that it is *not* a consequence of biological difference. No further clues are given as to its origin, character, or foundation.

Millett's book was received with great excitement by the Australian women's movement. Her concept of patriarchy, and her insistence on its cross-class character, was attractive to a movement founded on the assumption that women's oppression spanned class and on a desire for sisterhood and an autonomous women's movement. 'Patriarchy' gave a name to Friedan's 'problem that has no name'. Unlike the early terms 'women's oppression' and 'sexism', it could be made to refer to an entire social system. It was a theoretical concept which correlated with the growing political detachment of women's liberation from the New Left, and the movement's independence from working-class organisational structures and political institutions. It permitted a non-marxist identification of the issues at hand. For marxists in the women's movement, it became a problematic concept, at once attractive and yet difficult to reconcile with marxist analyses of class exploitation and differences.

But in these early years the problems surrounding the concept of patriarchy were not really confronted. Marxist and radical feminists were still united by a shared notion of 'women's oppression'. Both participated in the same groups and activities, embracing collective notions of political organisation. Both favoured small unstructured groups, working with a minimum of formality. The women from the New Left were only too pleased to escape the structured formality of Left groupings, the systems of office bearers, the endless motions, formal debates and procedural squabbles. And those from outside the Left often favoured a style of political meeting and action which did not adhere to formal meeting procedure, speaking before large groups, and so on. The style of organisation, then, had more affinities with anarchist traditions and perspectives than with either the Left or traditional meeting and organisational procedure. These early years seem now to have been an age of innocence, of belief in the possibility of sisterhood, of exciting discoveries, new groups and friendships. The emphasis was on ideological struggle, attitudinal change, and political protest designed to force changes in legislation and state action.

The development of marxist and radical feminism, 1972–81

Australian feminists found themselves confronted with some major changes in the 1972–75 period: the election of a Labor government in December 1972, the onset of recession in 1974 with growing unemployment, and the influence of academic marxism and other work from academic feminists. Each of these changes was important for the development of feminist theory and practice.

At the level of direct political action, the Labor government posed new problems which were in fact very old problems: what was the role of the state? The election of a Labor government made the possibility of effective state action seem more real. The newly established self-help centres such as health centres, rape crisis services, refuges, and childcare cooperatives had a good chance of securing government funding. The old revolution/reform dichotomy now had to be confronted, and a more precise strategy had to be worked out. The problem was incorporation and government control; the promise was effective action here and now to combat or at least relieve some aspects of 'women's oppression'. Some, for example, in the Women's Electoral Lobby, entered wholeheartedly into the attempt to influence the 'bureaucracy' to support services for women. Others, in the women's liberation groups, were more reluctant, but in the end many sought state funding for the self-help services they had initiated.

Soon after the demise of the Labor government, Rosemary Pringle and Ann Game provided an acute analysis of what had happened.[10] In both WEL and women's liberation there was a conception of a 'male power structure' which could be infiltrated or influenced or forced to make concessions. Pringle and Game argued that this conception forgets that the state is a mechanism for the maintenance of the political dominance of the 'capitalist class' over other classes. This failure to recognise the class basis of the state stemmed from a world view which saw 'sex oppression' as an independent structure, as 'prior to and providing the foundation for all other sorts of oppression'. In a capitalist society, however, sexism could not be seen as standing outside class relations, for these penetrate all social and political relations. Despite this perspective, Pringle and Game supported the decision to seek government funding, mainly on the grounds that the confrontation with the 'organisational forms and role of state intervention' had the potential to increase political (by which I think they largely meant class) awareness.

Pringle and Game's arguments were not, in general, taken up by the women's movement. The emphasis on 'male power' before 'class power' continued. Their analysis, however, was a pertinent one, and can be extended. In general, we might agree that while the state operates ultimately to secure.capitalist development, it does not do so in a simple way. It becomes an arena not only of class domination but also of class struggle. This includes not only struggles between classes, but also within them. In this case, we are looking at a struggle going on essentially *within* social classes, that is, a gender struggle within each class, but especially within the middle class. In this situation, women of each class seek to secure state action for support of their own aims. But it does not stop there, for the feminist analysis which asserts the common oppression of all women lays a basis for many middle-class women seeking reforms directed not only to the improvement of their own position relative to middle-class men, but also to the improvement of the position of working-class women overall.

Different political strategies ensued. Some aimed to achieve changes through entering the state bureaucracy itself, on behalf of working-class women; others concentrated on building cross-class political movements using a variety of protest and pressure-group tactics. Some sought government funding for feminist services, and thereby an increased state intervention, while others worked to reduce state intervention, at least in its law-and-order functions (for example, campaigns seeking the release of women prisoners). In different ways, then, feminist demands on the state are directed towards reordering gender relations within classes, strengthening the hand of middle- and working-class women in relation to that of men, especially from their own class.

Thus feminism is interwoven with both intra- and inter-class relations, and with the role of the state in regulating these relations. Feminism has the effect of politicising middle-class women towards an understanding of the specific forms of exploitation and oppression of working-class women. But it does not necessarily lead to an understanding of how class and racial exploitation affects men. The greater awareness of class exploitation and the class basis of state power which Pringle and Game hoped for has not, in general, occurred. Indeed, a stress on a class analysis, and on the marxist tradition which largely sustains it, has become increasingly unpopular within the women's movement, even among those women in it who are members of the Communist Party.[11]

The Labor government provided one source of change in direction for the women's movement which, around 1976, had dropped the term 'women's liberation'. A second source of change was the entry of feminist theory into the academy; academic theorists were beginning to influence the development of feminist theory. This was signified in 1973 by the inauguration of the journal *Refractory Girl*, and later, *Hecate*, and later still by the Women and Labour Conferences of 1978, 1980 and 1982. Another sign was the establishment of women's studies courses from about 1973. Feminists who had formerly regarded their academic work as separate from their feminist activity now came to see the two as part of a single process. One area of feminist debate and analysis to be especially influenced by this change was the sexual division of labour. Philosophers, sociologists, historians, and economists all delved into this problem.

Discussions of the sexual division of labour revealed a continuing marxist influence. The kind of marxism brought to bear on the problem was influenced strongly by the work of the Althusserians. In Britain, Selma James and Maria Dalla Costa argued that since the family maintained and reproduced labour power, and since labour power creates surplus value, then there must be a connection between domestic labour and the production of surplus value.[12] It was unclear whether they thought housework *produced* surplus value, or was simply necessary for the production elsewhere of surplus value, but they had opened a hornet's nest. The political consequence of this argument was a small but active movement for a brief period demanding wages for housework. A theoretical result was what has become known as the 'domestic-labour debate'. Because of the jargon, dryness, and difficulty of this debate, it was rejected as irrelevant by most feminist activists.

The Australian version of the debate, conducted in *Refractory Girl* and the *Journal of Australian Political Economy*, drew heavily on the British and Canadian arguments. Mia Campioni and her associates argued that domestic labour was indirectly productive of surplus value, and thereby exploited in the capitalist sense.[13] Brennan in contrast stated that full-time domestic labour represents a loss, not a saving, for capital: male wages have to be higher, and the labour supply is restricted, further increasing the price of labour.[14] For these reasons the 'family wage' principle, in so far as it was attained, was a victory for labour, and meant furthermore that working-class women did not have to do two exploited jobs, only one.

Both arguments had serious flaws, for each cast their net too narrowly. The first argument rests on a shaky understanding of the (in any case inadequate) labour theory of value, the second relies on a static conception of the content and character of domestic labour itself and of its relation to women's waged labour. But from all the debate, several conclusions emerged. In essence, most writers returned not to Morton's or Dalla Costa's formulations, but to Benston's, namely that housework produces use values (goods and services for immediate use) and not surplus value within the capitalist mode of production. Domestic labour was generally agreed to be indispensable *for* the capitalist mode of production, but not a part *of* it.[15]

Apart from its general impenetrability, the debate suffers from three problems: first, it said little about domestic labour outside the working class; second, it rested on a labour theory of value that could not be genderised as we see from Veronica Beechey's unsuccessful effort;[16] and third, it did not ask or answer the question 'why are *women* the domestic labourers?' It did not say why sexual division exists in capitalist societies or indeed at all. The debate was narrowly conceived, and has since been the basis of the claim that marxism has little of relevance to say to problems in feminist theory. But it is important to realise that only one aspect of the entire marxist tradition—that to do directly with the labour theory of value—was being used.

Gradually, interest in discussions of the sexual division of labour moved away from the domestic-labour debate and towards an understanding of women's waged labour. As the recession of the middle 1970s continued, there was an increasing awareness of the effects of technological change on the availability of work and on the nature of the work that remained. Following Harry Braverman, analyses appeared concentrating on deskilling and restructuring.[17] This work outlined the way the principle of a sexual division of labour was maintained under new conditions, while its details altered.[18] The focus on the family as a basis for sexual division in the workforce continued, with an increased emphasis on part-time work as a means of managing, but not solving, the contradiction for women between domestic responsibilities and the wages paid work brings. At a practical political level, this concern was manifested in a number of ways. There was support for legislation on equal employment opportunity. The trade union movement itself became active, especially through bodies such as the Melbourne Working Women's Centre under the auspices of the ACTU.[19] Feminism served as a galvanising force in sections of the trade union movement, and was partly responsible for increased union involvement of women, especially in skilled occupations such as nursing, teaching, banking, and social work. To some degree, this involvement did not hinge on the precise analysis given for women's disadvantages in the workforce. But in a larger sense, the analysis did matter, for the degree to which class or gender was emphasised affected the nature of work in unions, according to whether male unionists were seen as potential allies or implacable enemies.

Another, and probably numerically larger element of the women's movement was concerned with questions of male violence against women, especially rape, domestic violence, and pornography. Activism related to these issues was closely linked to a growing theoretical analysis. Two of the central theoretical contributions in this area came from the US: Susan Brownmiller's *Against Our Will: Men, Women, and Rape*, and Mary Daly's *Gyn/Ecology: The Meta-Ethics of Radical Feminism*.[20] Neither work bore any trace of the New Left origins of women's liberation, nor of the marxist strand of feminism. Both are, interestingly, works of history, aiming to show the longevity of male violence against women. Both leap from period to period and from culture to culture in pursuit of their assertion that men as a group use violence to exercise power over women as a group. The contexts, forms, and expressions of this violence change, but its essential purpose—the assertion and maintenance of power—does not. In the end there is no explanation for the horrific events and practices they describe other than the 'male will to power and control'. Brownmiller coined the famous statement that rape 'is nothing more nor less than a conscious process of intimidation by which *all men* keep *all women* in a state of fear'. The reasons for this are not given, and more attention is paid to explaining why there are laws against rape (protection of male property) than to why it occurs. Pornography, prostitution, the ideology of the heroic rapist and of women wanting to be raped, and basic male contempt for women are all outlined as contributing factors, but ultimately rape is given not so much a history as an anti-history, a timeless sequence in which men's contempt for and desire to humiliate, degrade, and control women is endlessly expressed.

Daly represents one pole of feminist thinking. She sees women and men as two orders of being and takes to its logical conclusion the notion of sexual oppression as the basis of all oppression. To Daly, no men are oppressed: all women are. Colonialism, imperialism, class exploitation—all cease to exist or matter. Militarism is a product only of male aggression and power play. So too are the ecological disasters of the modern world. The cornerstone of this world view is the notion of patriarchy, in its simplest form:

> ... women continue to be intimidated by the label anti-male. Some feel a need to draw false distinctions, for example: 'I am anti-patriarchal but not anti-male'. The courage to be logical—the courage to name—would require that we admit to ourselves that males and males only are the originators, planners, controllers, and legitimators of patriarchy. Patriarchy is the homeland of males; it is Father Land, and men are its agents.[21]

Daly's analysis reinstates men, all men, as the enemy.

Daly's work denies any salience to divisions other than gender. It ignores a class analysis absolutely. It also abandons any attempt to answer that initial feminist question—why do sexual division, inequality and power struggles occur?

The strongly radical feminist sector of the women's movement is not united within itself, as the pages of the Sydney-based radical feminist newspaper, *Girls' Own*, testify. Issues of debate include such fundamental matters as relations with men (both personal and political), lesbianism and heterosexuality, relations with male children, and separatism. But Daly's influence can be seen in its pages, as in Kimberley O'Sullivan's article in No. 5, 1981. O'Sullivan argues that the source of women's oppression is indeed biological: 'Wimmin and men are two different species. Not different races within the one humanoid species but different species who evolved separately and differently ... Wimmin are biologically and morally superior but men hold power by force of arms.' She goes on to say that all men are the same, that she loathes *all* of them, and that in her ideal world men will not exist. 'Wimmin will reproduce by parthenogenesis presumably.'

Given these divergent developments, which signify a major rupture within feminism itself, where can feminism go? In particular what do we now do with Millett's concept of patriarchy? What implications does its acceptance and use have for political practice? Does a concern to understand and combat 'patriarchy' involve a need for certain marxist concepts, or a need to refute them?

Marxism and the theory of patriarchy, 1978-83

Within marxist feminism, the concept of patriarchy had been widely accepted by the end of the decade as the theoretical debate became ever more abstract and jargon-ridden. Basically, the problem was that the marxists had accepted the radical feminist notion of patriarchy, but wanted to do something more marxist with it, to take it beyond Millett's level of description into the realm of explanation. The concept had to be transformed to represent a structure having a material base. Rowbotham, who later abandoned the attempt, was typical in arguing that 'patriarchal authority is based on male control over the woman's productive capacity, and over her person'.[22] The material base, then, lay not in the mode of production, nor in Firestone's reproductive duality, but in men's desire and ability to exercise control over women's sexuality, reproductive and productive capacities. This is not, in the end, a material base at all, and is itself something requiring further explanation.

Marxist feminist attempts to provide a marxist account of patriarchy are foundering on an inability to make 'patriarchy' itself a workable concept. In recent years this has been increasingly recognised. There are several possible responses to the theoretical impasse. One is to reject marxism as useful for understanding sexual division. This is the position taken by Hartmann and developed in Australia in several articles in Judith Allen and Paul Patton's *Beyond Marxism? Interventions After Marx*. Allen argues that patriarchy must be understood independently, without any necessary reference to other social divisions and relations, or other social theories. Marxism is identified as a unified, economic-determinist, 'productionist' body of thought which is generally useless for understanding sexual division. The result is that patriarchy will be found to have its own history, in which the differences between capitalist and non-capitalist forms of society may be found to be of little significance.[23]

Another way out of the theoretical impasse is to reject the concept of patriarchy, a position I've argued for elsewhere, on the grounds that it presumes at the start the conclusions of the analysis of the operations of gender and sexual division. The degree to which being male rather than female brings with it cultural value and power varies across societies, historical periods, and social classes;

whatever the degree, it needs to be demonstrated rather than assumed.

Yet another is to reject both the concept of patriarchy *and* the possibility that marxism might be useful for understanding the nature of sexual division. This position is probably best represented in the British journal *m/f*, I am not aware of any extensive Australian counterpart. Writers in *m/f* argue that the concept of 'patriarchy' imposes a false unity on what is in fact a series of competing and historically specific discourses and social practices constructing 'men' and 'women'. These writers also reject marxism as a possible approach, seeing it much as Judith Allen does. The result is a rejection of the entire debate so far, and a combination of impressive critiques of existing theories with a less than impressive construction of alternative approaches. The question of determination, which has occupied feminists in various camps, is effectively set aside.

Finally there is the view that a theory of patriarchy and a version of marxism are in fact compatible. In Australia, this is best represented in Game and Pringle's *Gender at Work*.[24] The authors argue that capitalism is a form of patriarchy, a form in which a sexual division of labour is built in, as a defining feature. But to my mind they have no means of explaining why this might be so. They argue that capitalism rests on a production/consumption split, but do not ask why women were and are more identified with consumption and men with production.

So the Marxist tradition has not yet come to grips with the problem of explaining why sexual division occurs, why for example it is *women* who generally do unpaid domestic labour and childcare. But then, neither has the radical feminist tradition provided any explanations. While more focused on the problem 'why is it *women* who . . . ?', their answers have been either circular, tautologous, or merely descriptive, *or* have taken refuge in the assertion of men's desire to control women.

Conclusion

As a general point, I think we need to do two things. First, we need to keep our attention focused on the problem of explanation, to refuse to slip into an assertive descriptiveness. Second, we need to cease searching for *one single* principle of explanation, a magic phrase like 'men's desire to control women' or 'women's identification with motherhood' to explain it all. In searching for explanations we need a framework which rejects 'patriarchy' as an independent area of analysis.

Nor can we simply replace 'patriarchy' with the notion of a 'sex/gender' system, as some writers suggest. Most notably, Gayle Rubin in her well-known essay 'The Traffic in Women: Notes on the "Political Economy" of Sex', argued for the notion of a 'sex/gender system', hoping that it would enable feminist theorists to maintain an open mind on whether there really was male dominance in any particular situation.[25] In the same vein, Jill Matthews more recently argued in *Good and Mad Women* that a useful concept was that of a 'gender order', which she defines as 'a systematic process of power relations' which creates social women and men and orders the patterns of relations among and between them. It is thus conceivable that these relations could be equitable, and Matthews makes the point that whether they are or not 'cannot be assumed but must be proven for each specific society'.[26] Yet she somewhat undermines her case by stating, without argument or evidence, that all gender orders so far have been hierarchical, inequitable, and oppressive, with the masculine as superior to and dominating of the feminine.

The main problem with the attempt by Rubin, Matthews, and many others to devise theoretical categories which do not foreclose discussion in the way that patriarchy as a concept seems to do, is that they adhere to the idea of a single sex/gender system within a given society, and thereby to the notion that the relations between men and women, as socially constituted, are systematic. But it may be that the significance of gender as an organising principle is inconsistent, unsystematic, and multivalent. Given the constant intrusion into gender-related matters of other forms of social division and structure, it seems indeed highly likely that this will be so.

Just as racism and race relations cannot be adequately understood without reference to the contexts within which they occur, neither can sexism and sexual division. In both cases, a sense of biological identity is socially produced, but not on the basis of a neutral, undifferentiated body. In both cases the social meanings attributed to these biological recognitions will depend on the nature of the social structure producing them.

In this sense, we should return to Firestone's interest in the biological duality in human reproduction, not as a justification or explanation for sexual inequality and division, but as a starting point for understanding what it is that is being socially elaborated. Then the analysis will depend on the kind of society under discussion. Ours is a capitalist society, with complexities of class relations, political and legal structure, and colonial heritage. Sexual division is produced within and by that capitalist society and cannot be understood independently of it.

Throughout this paper I have been arguing that there is a connection between feminist theory, feminist practice, and the social base of feminist movements. It is possible to confine one's concern to social justice for women, but in doing so, the most we can hope for is to reorder gender relationships within social classes, or within racial or ethnic groups. The bases for class or racial exploitation are left relatively undisturbed. Further, regarding the demand for social justice for women as an independent demand can lead to a situation where relatively privileged women seek to advance their own position further over that of relatively unprivileged men. The search for institutionalised power and wealth are, in this perspective, endorsed when it is women who seek them. Only a feminism deeply aware of forms of oppression and exploitation other than gender can avoid this pitfall.

Australian feminism has included both kinds of approaches: those which isolate an understanding of sexual division and a demand for social justice for women, and those that combine feminism with the search for justice for other disadvantaged groups. But there has been a general drift towards isolation, in terms both of understanding and political practice. It is time to remember the New Left origins of the modern Australian women's movement, to recover some of that neglected concern with the problems of capitalism, imperialism, and class exploitation. If we focus on social justice for women as something which has been independently produced and can be independently achieved, we forget the larger context which, I would argue, both produces sexual inequality and power relations, and the possibility of their demise.

PART V

Theorising women, work, and family

14

Women and class

Soon after the conference on Women and Social Justice, I developed, in a paper to the Marxist Summer School in Sydney in January 1984, my argument on the issue of women and class. My paper attracted a long discussion. There was energetic support and equally energetic opposition. I have incorporated into the last part of this version, in the discussion of socialist feminism, some additional material written at around the same time.

1984

Views of society based on a contrast of the position of 'women' with that of 'men' have a different way of organising our understanding of social life than do views which rest on a notion of class division. Feminists and socialists have different starting points. Yet socialists have had to come to terms with issues of sexual inequality, while feminists are faced with the problem that while they posit a common 'oppression of women', they must recognise also the very great differences between women according to their social class. This problem is not a new one for feminism. It bedevilled First Wave feminists, especially those attracted to socialist ideals and organisations. It bedevils modern feminism. No matter how exhaustively and endlessly feminists discuss it, the issues raised under the heading 'women and class' continue to emerge as important and problematic.

Until about four or five years ago, I did not, actually, find it especially a problem. I would argue that women's oppression and class exploitation were both deeply embedded in our society, and that one had to take both into account, seeing a complex inter-relationship. In practice my analyses concentrated on working-class women, for here both systems of domination could be seen to be operating. In the area of the sexual division of labour, for example, one could suggest how the identification of women, and not men, with childcare formed a basis for a sexual division in the workforce which in turn reinforced that identification.

But around 1981 I began to find these formulations inadequate. The often-heard charge—that the women's movement is essentially a middle-class phenomenon—which I had earlier dismissed as a basically sexist attempt to dismiss the importance of the women's movement and the issues it raises, I now began to take more seriously. I was influenced, I suppose, by my changing social environment. As I grew older, and gained greater job security and a higher level of pay, I saw my feminist friends around me experiencing the same process. We were the first post-Hiroshima generation, the baby-boom generation, who had experienced the educational expansion and the plentiful job supply of the 1960s. Now, by the early 1980s, we were in our mid- to late thirties, had completed our education and training, gone through the difficult early years of uncertain employment, and had become established. We became public servants, journalists, teachers, academics, librarians, social workers, and so on. We published magazines, saw the correct films, attended the correct meetings, and had consciousness-raised ourselves to think correct thoughts. We were more often than not mortgaged to the hilt buying houses, and many of us had travelled for a time overseas. We became the kind of people who were asked to give papers at conferences, and had at last acquired sufficient confidence to do so. The women's movement which we had helped to build had given us much: a perspective, moral support, friendships, and an avenue through which we could act for social and political change.

The women I'm speaking of were, then, in terms of the society they lived in, highly privileged people. They had been born at the right time, had had access to education, and now had a relatively high degree of job security and material comfort. Yet how did this group, these friends of mine in the women's movement, see themselves? They saw themselves as oppressed, as victims, as underdogs. They would complain bitterly about the pain of being women, about the men they worked with or knew, about relationships. They would go to all-women parties and conferences, and complain. My God how they whinged! Life was a dreary round of problems and defeats, pain and disillusion. As they drank their pretty good wine (no more of the red rot-gut of student days) and helped themselves to magnificent food, they told themselves how much they were suffering the pain of being women. They recognised their material advantages in some ways, but at bottom identified themselves as part of an oppressed group—women. As their conversational diet moved from relationships and exams and lectures, through to relationships, children (or alternatively how horrible children were), and divorces, and through again to relationships, mortgages and renovations, operations and female diseases, their underlying theme was their own oppression.

Around 1981, the contradictions in all this suddenly overwhelmed me. How self-indulgent this all was! How closed, how spoilt, how pampered! These women might ironically refer to themselves as the 'spoilt generation' but they seemed unable to recognise how spoilt they were. And I began to wonder how this was possible. For the people I'm talking about regarded themselves as socialists of some kind, as opposed to capitalism, to Malcolm Fraser (Prime Minister at the time), to imperialism, to the nuclear arms race. If most were not marxists in any very serious sense, then most were at least aware of class exploitation and the ways it is produced under capitalism. How could socialists so easily identify themselves, the relatively privileged, as oppressed? How could socialists have become so blind to the exploitation and struggles of working-class and/or colonised men? How had they come to identify the relative privilege and power of the middle-class men they combated in their working lives with the position of all men?

One answer, of course, is feminism. Feminism, even in its most class-aware pro-socialist varieties, had enabled these women to blind themselves to where so much privilege lay. It enabled them to locate themselves on the side of the oppressed, and working-class men as at least the collaborators with, but more likely as themselves among, the oppressors. And so I began to think that some very basic questioning of feminist propositions was needed. I began to think that the categories 'women' and 'men', as so commonly used in feminist discourse, needed some deconstructing. It seemed to me that what had in the early 1970s begun, for us, as a very necessary analysis—namely that the individual problems many of us experienced were in fact products of social distinctions and structures—had developed into an absurd level of generalisation. Women feel or think such and such, men don't, and so on.

But if the categories needed deconstructing, then there was the problem of not throwing out the baby with the bathwater. I didn't want to go back to the earlier Left sects' denial of the importance of the issues feminism raised. I didn't want to reject feminism on the grounds that it split the Left, that all would come good after the revolution. I didn't want to return to a situation where issues like rape, domestic violence, abortion, sexuality, sexual exploitation and harassment, the sexual division of labour, notions of masculinity and femininity, housework and childcare, and all the rest were legislated back off the radical agenda. Not that they ever had been entirely absent from it, especially in the cases of equal pay and childcare, but they hadn't been very firmly on it either. I recognised that the women's movement had achieved something of profound importance in creating all these as issues, and in pursuing them through trade union, state, and other institutional, ideological, and cultural channels. So the problem was, for me, how to retain these very real gains and insights, and yet restore a more truly socialist awareness of the manifest and hidden injuries of class. How, that is, could we return to that older socialist problem of the possibilities for middle-class support of a working-class revolution?

The issues seemed complicated for a particular reason. This was how to understand the changing class structure and nature of capitalism itself. One strand of thought was to argue that the people I've here been referring to as 'middle-class' are actually the upper layers of the working class. They earn a wage, they have nothing, more or less, to sell but their labour power. If they lose their jobs, they face poverty (perhaps after a time) like anyone else. This seems to me useful, for there is indeed no basis for these salaried members of the 'middle class', or in some arguments the 'new middle class', being regarded as structurally distinct from the working class. Rather, what we have is a large working class, internally stratified. Yet if we accept this form of analysis, we need also to accept that within this large working class, the differences in job security, rates of pay, and access to positions of institutional power, are vast. It is politically important, I think, for teachers, academics, social workers, journalists, and public servants to define themselves as workers, and to develop a trade-union and political consciousness accordingly. It is equally important, though, not to lose sight of the fact that such groups of people are significantly privileged in contrast with the bulk of the working class. While it is true that many groups formerly thought of as 'middle-class'—such as clerical workers— have been proletarianised, it is also true that the having or not of the kind of skills which can earn a secure and interesting job and a reasonable wage is still a profound source of differentiation among the non-owners of this society. Educational qualifications, in particular, still count a great deal. And this differentiation is made even sharper by the fact that unemployment hits the unskilled by far the hardest.

A second common way of thinking about how the class structure of advanced capitalist societies has changed has been to say that, given the postwar advances in the pay and conditions of employed working-class people, the real oppressed are not the working class per se, but special categories, sometimes referred to as the marginals. These groups include women, Aborigines, non-English-speaking migrants, prisoners, the unemployed. Any employed

Anglo-Australian male is thereby deemed as not to be exploited, no matter how tedious, insecure, or low-paying his job may be. The argument is that this male employed working class has been bought off, and no hope for radical change can be found there. The institutional creations of this group—the trade unions—are to be dismissed as conservative, racist, sexist, etc. without any real reference to whether they are Left or Right, or what kind of politics they pursue.

Such a view has certain strengths. It points to the ways the working class is divided, and to bases for social inequality and domination other than class. It recognises the degree to which trade unions lie in danger of incorporation, cooption, and collaboration. But it has some key weaknesses too. It fails to see how many of these specific oppressions are tied in with the class nature of capitalism, that they acquire the character they do as a result of: colonialism (in the case of Aborigines); the uneven distribution of capital bringing forth a necessity for the international mobility of labour (in the case of migrants); the repressive role of the capitalist state (in the case of prisoners); the inability of capitalism in periods of recession to provide jobs for all (in the case of the unemployed); and the fact that capitalism rests on a particular family structure whereby domestic labour and childcare are only partly drawn into the wages system (in the case of women). The analysis fails to see that many of the so-called marginals are in fact working-class, whether they are employed or not. It fails to see also that *some* people within these special categories—such as middle-class women and better-off NES migrants—have considerable resources with which to combat the specific discriminations and inequalities they experience. What it does is to move from a very necessary recognition of conflict and diversity within the working class and within other classes to a denial of the validity of class itself. It forgets how capitalism works, how it is based on fundamental distinctions between capital and labour, owners and non-owners, managers and workers, and secures its hegemony through the provision of grossly differential material rewards and degrees of control and power to the populations who sustain it.

There is another factor affecting degrees of privilege and perceptions of it. And that is age, especially as it affects those I have described as in the upper strata of the working class. Life for the young members of that group is not a bed of roses. Students are very often exceptionally poor. Many of the students I teach do not eat properly, and live in grossly overcrowded and run-down shared houses. Entering the job market is not easy, even when you have marketable skills. It is only after a period of time that the benefits incurred from having those skills start to be realised. It is partly for this reason, I think, that so many radical movements depend for their troops on young people in the process of acquiring professional skills—people who experience immediate difficulties but who have the freedom which flows from an awareness of a long-term future. For young people not undergoing this process of preparation for salaried secure jobs, the spectre and reality of unemployment, and the knowledge that any long-term security will be an exceedingly hard battle, very often militate against organised political radicalism. For women what this difference means is that whereas young women in the less privileged sections of the working class devote enormous energies to establishing a marriage, and saving for a house and so on, young women from its privileged sections devote similar energies to acquiring skills, resisting marriage, family, house-buying and so on, and seeking a lifestyle which allows space for alternatives, and in many cases for political and cultural activity.

And so I get back to feminism. Why do the relatively privileged women I began by discussing become blinded to the fact of their own privilege, and the lack of it in many working-class men? Why are sexual inequalities seen not so much as complicating the effects of class exploitation but as replacing it altogether? I've suggested several answers. The concept of 'women's oppression' allows them to define themselves as victims, however relatively privileged they may be. The extension of the category working class to include salaried, higher-paid workers allows us to forget the very real differences in material rewards and access to power within that working class. The politics of special categories of oppression obscures a recognition of class differentiation within some of those categories—especially women and migrants—and so obscures an understanding of capitalism as resting on class exploitation.

We need to recognise that the differences in class and sub-class position between women deeply affect responses to feminism. These differences are, I think, based on women's differing perceptions of the position of men in their own class, or sub-class. Women from the more privileged sections of the working class see their male equivalents as having levels of wealth and power which are denied to the women on the basis of sexual discrimination and the realities of a sexist society generally. They battle with these men for a more equal share of the cake: job opportunities, career paths, levels of pay, and influence in policy-making within public and private organisations. Women from the rest of the working class do not, on the whole, see it this way. They see the men of their own section of the working class as exploited, as not earning enough to support a family at the desired level, if they are earning at all.

Such women frequently seek work opportunities and greater rights and remuneration in the workplace and thus a greater measure of material comfort and financial independence for themselves where possible. They also seek greater negotiating power within a family context. But they do not perceive themselves as locked in a battle with men for these things, and will, when questioned, assume that men have greater rights to a full-time secure job than they themselves have. They see themselves struggling for husbands to get secure jobs, themselves to work where they can and be sufficiently supported if they cannot; for a reasonable material level; and for alternatives if the everlasting battle for secure family life is temporarily or permanently lost. To the extent that feminism provides them with the weapon to achieve their aims they welcome it, but a feminism which describes 'men' as the enemy does not speak to their situation.

I do not think the feminist critique of the family is attractive to these less privileged working-class women; what most of them seek is adequate conditions for securing family life. It is for more privileged women, on the whole, that rejection of family life has proved an attractive option. And the reasons, though complex, have one clear element: such a rejection is more feasible if you can expect, on the basis of recognised skills, to earn a reasonable wage throughout your adult life. There may, of course, be periods of unemployment, especially now and especially for younger women, but by and large your chances of self-support—and thereby your interest in transient (communal) rather than semi-durable (family) households—are heavily conditioned by your class position.

So feminism needs to come to terms more than I think it has with several basic features of social life under capitalism: with the differing positions and therefore relation to feminism of women in different classes and sub-classes, with the very real exploitation of less privileged working-class men, with the problems of building working-class unity in a society which hands out its benefits and rewards so grossly unequally.

Socialist feminists need, I think, to remember more strongly than many of them do the production of inequalities other than those based on sex or gender. Many have based themselves on a radical feminist ideology more deeply than most might care to recognise. Their acceptance of a radical feminist framework is signified by an adoption of the radical feminist use of the concepts 'women's oppression' and 'patriarchy'. At a theoretical level the work of the British marxist feminist Michele Barrett, entitled *Women's Oppression Today*, illustrates the problem well.[1] The title tells the story. Barrett criticises many radical feminist positions from a marxist perspective, but her simultaneous adherence to a radical feminist framework results in confusion.

In any case, many marxist feminists have gradually dropped the 'marxist' and retained the 'feminist'. There has been a steady stream of previous marxist feminists rejecting the usefulness of marxism. As time goes on, one after another of former marxist feminists has announced her conviction that the two theories can not be integrated or made compatible, and that if a choice has therefore to be made it has to be for feminism. Hopes for an integrated theory have gradually dwindled and died. This rejection of the usefulness of marxism for feminist theory has had dire consequences for feminist politics. We are now confronted with the anomaly that many socialist feminists talk constantly about 'men' and 'women' in non-class-differentiated ways, refuse to cope with the fact that upper- and middle-class women are privileged in this society and in world terms, and evince—in my experience—remarkably little empathy or political allegiance with working-class men.

Many middle-class women, in fighting for their own interests, forget that they may be bringing into being another instance of class privilege. This is easier to see historically than in the present. Everything always is. Certainly we can see how the First Wave feminists were usually enmeshed in the problems of their own class, seeking property rights, and political representation, were interested in eugenics, getting enough servants, and so on. We can applaud and identify with their struggles against the men of their own class, but we cannot so easily applaud their approaches to working-class men and women.

Many middle-class women today think they have avoided this by identifying their interests with those of working-class women, by establishing a new wave of social services for women, or by constantly pointing to the double or triple burden of working-class women. But this isn't good enough. My point is: what about working-class men? As long as middle-class women identify them as part of the enemy, the oppressors, and cast themselves as the oppressed, they have a theoretical basis for continuing to exert class privilege, for asserting their own interests over those of working-class men. And for socialists, marxists, this just won't do. Which is not to say one doesn't combat sexism wherever one finds it—in trade unions, or wherever. It is to say that to focus on sexism out of context, to remain wilfully blind to the realities of class privilege and exploitation in this way, must locate a class-blind feminism as politically reactionary.

It is only when these issues are grappled with seriously that feminist critiques and analyses and demands—most if not all of which I regard as profoundly important—will be able to be fought for in a way which not only reorders gender relations within classes but also reorders class relationships altogether.

15

The family and feminism

Among other things, the paper on women and class had continued the critique of the feminist view of the family that I'd begun in 'Radical Feminism' in 1982. I developed these ideas a little further in a review essay I wrote for Hecate *in 1985 on a group of books, British and Australian, on the family. These included Lynne Segal (ed.)* What is to be Done About the Family? Crisis in the Eighties *(Harmondsworth 1983); Michele Barrett and Mary McIntosh* The Anti-Social Family *(London 1982); Betsy Wearing* The Ideology of Motherhood: A Study of Sydney Suburban Mothers *(Sydney 1984); and Ferdinand Mount* The Subversive Family: An Alternative History of Love and Marriage *(London 1982). A revised version of the review appears below.*

1985

Modern feminism has been deeply critical of the family, by which it means the nuclear family household. The 'oppression of women' has been held to be based on women's confinement to, dependence on, and control by men within that family. As early as 1970 Kate Millett linked the family to the juggernaut of 'patriarchy' as it began its journey (slowly at first) through feminist theory:

> Patriarchy's chief institution is the family. It is both a mirror of and a connection with the larger society; a patriarchal unit within a

patriarchal whole ... Revolutionary or utopian efforts to remove these functions [socialisation and reproduction] from the family have been so frustrated, so beset by difficulties, that most experiments so far have involved a gradual return to tradition. This is strong evidence of how basic a form patriarchy is within all societies, and of how pervasive its effects upon family members.[1]

Since Millett, the family has been seen as the basis for wider forms of women's oppression: their secondary and particularly exploited role in the labour market; their exclusion from much political and trade union activity and especially from high public office; their objectification within rather than their own creation of both high and popular culture.

Feminists point out that conventional family arrangements, in intimate conjunction with labour market inequalities, reduce the possibility of personal, bodily, and financial autonomy for women. Childbearing and rearing come to involve financial dependence, making it difficult for women to leave unsatisfactory, even violent, marriages. This economic inequality is disastrous for the power relations within families, and for those women who fall outside the family altogether.

Feminism also posits other, non-economic, problems with the nuclear family: a presumption of the 'normality' of heterosexuality and the 'deviance' of homosexuality; an over-intensity of relationships between only a few people; a creation of women as highly intensive mothers with few other connections with social, political, and economic life, leading to loneliness and to a neurotic obsessiveness with children; and the petty tyranny able to be practised by men convinced of their own superior rights on the basis of their sex and of their earning power.

On the basis of these critiques of the family, feminists have advocated both personal rejection of the nuclear family household, with the establishment of alternative living arrangements, and policies enabling women to escape that household: childcare services, job and pay equality, and increased possibilities for childlessness via access to contraception and abortion.

Yet the program of abolition of the family has proved troublesome for feminists, particularly in the growing recognition that it has been one of the less popular of feminist demands, and the one most vulnerable to concerted conservative attack. Feminists who themselves have children do not necessarily want to, or feel able to, reject the nuclear family household. The task of developing alternatives here and now has not proved altogether easy. There has been a slide from the earlier cry 'abolish the family' to 'greater choice in living and sexual arrangements', a slide which takes account of these problems but which robs the earlier demand and critique of much of its bite. Further, as the debate has proceeded, feminists have become more aware of the complexities of analysis—of the difficulties of working out how, why and when the nuclear family household arose, the mutual cause-and-effect relationship between family structures and the organisation of industrial capitalist production, and the dynamics of the formation of gendered identity within the family.

All of these except *The Subversive Family* reflect this increasing uncertainty and sense of complexity in feminist discussions of the family. If none of them is theoretically very satisfying, they nevertheless together provide welcome evidence that the theoretical debate and empirical research necessary for greater understanding of the issues involved is continuing. The dominant themes running through this very heterogeneous collection concern the relation between the nuclear family, household and 'women's oppression', and whether or not such households are 'selfish', 'anti-social'. For opponents of this kind of family, its anti-sociality and oppression of women are bound together; for supporters, both criticisms are denied.

Lynne Segal's edited collection is entitled *What is to be Done About the Family? Crisis in the Eighties*, a title aptly indicating socialist feminism's loss of certainty and direction in Thatcher's Britain. The book is founded on some key principles: alternative living arrangements are in general preferable to conventional family ones, though they have their problems and we shouldn't be too prescriptive; the dynamics of the family and indeed of alternatives to it depend on the wage inequalities produced by capitalism; and the key to change for the better lies in full employment, shorter working hours, and good childcare facilities. Thus feminist demands are firmly grounded in Left ones, though there is a noticeable distance from the trade union movement as a possible agent of change. There is also an ambivalence about the state as a provider of solutions, an ambivalence which is never fully sorted out.

It is the first three chapters that Australian readers can benefit from most, for although the British and the Australian movements have their differences there is enough similarity for the accounts of the 1960s and early 1970s to resonate. In particular Mica Nava's account of early feminist critiques of the family is lively, interesting, and informative, and brings back memories of the idealism of those years, the plans for anti-sexist alternative lifestyles. Lynne Segal's own chapter, on the 1960s libertarian and New Left critiques, is also refreshing and insightful, especially in her account of the unresolved tension between the desire for communal living and the profound individualism— the emphasis on personal fulfilment—of the New Left. This chapter, and indeed the rest of the book, is founded on a recognition of the importance of security, love, and friendship, the ties that bind and so run counter to individual freedom and autonomy. How can a feminism develop which recognises this? The book does not go much further than to pose the question. Despite its useful insights, *What is to be Done About the Family?* gives, overall, the impression that British feminist campaigning and theory have run into the ground. Apart from its coverage of some recent developments in feminist debate, for example a more pointed discussion—in the light of Thatcherite attacks—of women and the welfare state, little comes through by way of clear demands and proposals. The contributors are lively and illuminating on the past, foggy on the present, and bewildered about the future.

Michele Barrett and Mary McIntosh in *The Anti-Social Family* perceive the problem much as Segal and her contributors do: the needs the family answers (imperfectly) for love, commitment, and security should be able to be met outside the family, in wider social arrangements. For while the family does offer a means for meeting such needs, it is profoundly anti-social. Perhaps because it is a jointly authored book, rather than a collection, it offers a more coherent feminist critique than Segal's does of the family or, more precisely, of family-based households and the time, energy, and emotion commonly invested in them.

Barrett and McIntosh argue that the family persists, both as ideal and reality, for two main reasons. First, our economic and social structures make it difficult to establish alternatives—barriers include gender-based wage inequalities, current housing patterns, and the scarcity and cost of childcare facilities. But second, and more profoundly, we *think* the family is the natural and only way to meet our deepest emotional needs. We are victims of familial ideology, which not only surrounds us in explicit advocacy of family life but also permeates our entire culture, from the Royal Family to soap opera. While we need to change the economic and social structures impeding the development of alternatives, for Barrett and McIntosh the main task is to think our way out of the family. We need to reject its seduction, and recognise its anti-social and sexist character.

Barrett and McIntosh make several points to support their charge of anti-sociality. The family reproduces class inequality; our chances in life depend on the family that raises us. The family weakens community life and collectivism and leads to individualism, to a focus on private life. The family guarantees male power and female dependence. It becomes a prison for women, where they may have to submit to violence and rape, and to isolation in their little box-houses. Housework in the family-household context is done mainly by women and is long, boring, exhausting work. Mothering tends to exclude the possibility of other activities. The family is the site for gender inequality in general, where women get the worst end of the deal in terms of hours and tedium of work, less decision-making power in spending, and less sexual freedom.

In all this, Barrett and McIntosh seem to me to confuse a description of the character of many family-households with an argument as to its necessary effects. Let's go through their criticisms one by one. First, the family as a reproducer of class inequality. This is certainly true, but surely what is at issue here is not the family but class inequality. Is it at all clear that other kinds of living arrangements and other contexts for rearing children would lead to a looser fit between one's own class position and that of one's parents? Even if it did, this would entail only greater upward and downward mobility; it would not change class inequality itself. I would not have thought that social mobility was a particularly socialist demand.

Next there is the issue of the family weakening community life and collectivism. This is a very large claim, and I wonder a) whether it is true, and b) about the chicken-and-egg character of the argument. How weak *is* community and collective life in fact? Are those people living in family-household arrangements the most privatised, the least sociable, the least politically and culturally active? Do other arrangements necessarily imply greater communality? Privatisation and isolation seem to me to be genuine issues of concern, but I wonder whether family-household arrangements are their source. Surely other issues, such as the organisation of paid work, are relevant here.

Barrett and McIntosh then tackle the issue of the gender inequalities which exist within and are produced by the family. Here their critique is quite powerful, though it is not at all new. But again I wonder if the issue is the family household arrangement as such. Rather than focus on household arrangements, it would seem to be more basic to focus on the question of the economic dependence that mothering tends to bring. This confronts women no matter whether we live inside the conventional family structure or outside it, though the resolution to the problems posed by childcaring may differ. Family households do have many of the characteristics Barrett and McIntosh ascribe to them, but they do so not because parents and their children co-reside, but because of the particular consequences of childcaring in an industrial capitalist society.

This is then a curious book. While it seems to be a typical feminist critique, seeing the family as a basic site of women's oppression, on closer inspection it belongs rather to a much older utopian socialist and perhaps libertarian-anarchist tradition, discourses which oppose the family as the usurper of the properly social and communal. Yet throughout the book, its definition of community remains shadowy indeed.

Betsy Wearing's *The Ideology of Motherhood* is based on the view that an ideology which prescribes motherhood as sufficiently satisfying for women serves to limit the lives of women and to legitimate their overall subordination. She values lifestyles which can allow a combination of motherhood with other interests, and is critical of lifestyles where other interests either do not exist or cannot be pursued. Both poverty and traditional notions of women's place as mother are seen as restricting women's lives, bearing down most heavily on working-class women. Feminist networks and shared households are presented as having enabled feminist mothers to find genuine solutions to the problem of successfully combining motherhood with other activities.

Despite its rather prescriptive tone, and a fairly flat repetitive style, Wearing's book is ethnographically interesting. It is the result of research with three groups of Sydney mothers—working-class mothers at Mt Druitt, middle-class North Shore mothers, and middle-class feminist Balmain mothers. It is informative and insightful about the difference class makes to the conditions and experience of mothering and family life. Of particular interest is the detailed account of mothers' networks of kin, friends, and neighbours, which make mothering a much less isolated activity than feminist analyses (like Barrett and McIntosh's) usually assume. Wearing regards these networks, though, as 'good' only where they enable *escape* from mothering part of the time. Their importance as sociability and solidarity is in my view underestimated.

If Wearing is correct, then the usual picture of mothering–isolation, paid labour–conviviality, needs severe questioning. Many workplaces are small and many jobs do not in fact lead to great sociability. Reorganisation of work has made many workplaces unconvivial. And mothering may not in fact be as uniformly isolating as feminists suppose. Wearing's work is valuable in rescuing suburbs like Mt Druitt (in Sydney's west) from the usual sociological picture of them as isolated, alienated, each housewife in her own box-house, and providing us with a picture instead of healthy neighbourly and friendship ties.

Another valuable feature of Wearing's book is the discussion of the impact of feminist ideology on the experience of mothering. She shows that middle-class mothers, whether feminist or not, have the resources to lighten their work load and to pursue other interests. Their own car allows mobility, and they can attend classes, meetings, activity groups, or whatever. Feminist mothers are a subset of this group. They either have reasonable incomes or, if their income is low, they are usually in shared households and so gain from a good use of scarce resources. But where they are distinctive is that they have a feminist ideology and a feminist friendship and political network which jointly enable them to make mothering a sociable and not a limiting activity.

The portrayal of these networks is valuable, but I wonder

whether it is just a little too glowing. As one who experienced mothering of a young child with very few networks of support indeed, I carry the image of isolated mothering amidst a feminist milieu close to my heart. Far from finding feminist networks supportive, I found them quite the opposite. Sharing of childcare was practically unknown, and a less supportive atmosphere can scarcely be imagined. This flowed from the ideological opposition to mothering itself, and also from the fact that so few feminists had young children at all. Other feminist mothers have mentioned similar experiences to me; I feel the case for supportive feminist networks is not entirely proven.[2]

All three books lead one to conclude that there is a need to differentiate between two issues that feminists too frequently confuse. One is the question of household and kinship organisation; the other is the question of sexual inequality. Sexual inequality or equality is not dependent on household and kinship structures per se, on whether children live with one parent, or both, or with additional relatives, or additional non-related adults. It is dependent, rather, on the economic basis of that household, on the unpaid nature of the domestic work within a wages system, and on the authority relations between the adults in the household.

These books all engage with the issue of how, in feminist terms, we ought to live. In strong contrast is Ferdinand Mount's *The Subversive Family*. Mount was director of Margaret Thatcher's Policy Unit at the time of the book's publication. Its flavour is New Right, based on an opposition to the growth and intervention of the state, or at least the welfare state. Yet despite its exceptionally dubious political origins, and its sloppy, repetitive and scattered argument, this book makes points that both marxists and feminists could well consider.

The Subversive Family argues that the family, far from being the servant of the state portrayed in marxist feminist and other theory, is an institution which undermines it. Both church and state attempt, after a struggle, to incorporate the family, to grant it a 'high place in the orthodox dogma of ideology', but it is the family not the state which in the end sets the terms.

In presenting this case Mount provides a rather rough-and-ready account of debates among historians over the history of the family. He popularises the findings of researchers such as Peter Laslett of the Cambridge Group for the History of Population and Social Structure, findings which repudiate the common idea that the nuclear family is recent and fleeting, arguing instead that it is in fact a very old form of human cohabitation and effective institution. He repeats academic demolitions of Engels' evolutionary account of the family, and argues the opposite—that the nuclear family came first. His general purpose is to reinstate the notion that the nuclear family is the natural way of organising human relationships and residence patterns, by indicating its longevity and universality. To this point Mount has said nothing new, and his book has a tone of wild assertion. But towards the end he becomes more interesting. In chapter 9, 'The Family Haters', Mount argues that the charge of selfishness—that the family is inward-looking and a barrier to genuine communality—is a very old charge indeed. He races through the centuries, mentioning Plato, the Ranters of seventeenth-century England, Sir Edmund Leach, André Gide, the futurist Marinetti, and artists in general. His case is not well made; it is an interesting point nonetheless, revealing that feminist arguments, as we've already noticed in the case of Barrett and McIntosh, have a much older cultural and intellectual history. In chapter 10, 'Privacy and the Working Class', Mount defends the family on the grounds that here the working class achieves what it wants, not what it is told it ought to want by middle-class do-gooders. He attacks those versions of marxism which see the working class as 'helpless, passive, unconscious victims of huge economic and social processes', seeing an affinity between these views and the distaste for modern working-class culture expressed by D.H. Lawrence and F.R. Leavis. Against this Mount argues that 'the working class family provides, every day, its own living refutation of the accusation of passivity and manipulation' and further, 'ordinary people are quite capable of describing their position and defending it'. He defends the often-attacked desire for consumer durables on the grounds that they usually do in fact make life easier, and attacks the fashionable (with both Right and Left) mourning of the passing of the old sense of working-class community, the notion that people have become more isolated, and more like things. In contrast he argues that working-class people see more not less of their non-resident kin than they used to, as they have both more leisure and more mobility than in the past. He defends private life and attacks the interventionist state and its agents as 'public busybodies'. These are the working class's most dangerous enemies, for they are there to inspect and oversee and regulate as well as help.

So where does Mount's book lead us? One could read it simply as a highly conservative defence of the family, in which all manner of alternatives are rejected and opposed as 'unnatural'. On the other hand one could welcome the defence of modern working-class culture, and the argument against state intervention in the intimate details of people's lives. A problem for feminism is that all paths seem to lead to the state, as guarantor of feminist demands, as an alternative to the private tyranny of the family, and to the structured sexual inequality of the workplace. We might very well suspect Mount's motives, as seeking to justify a contraction of the welfare state; we need nevertheless to regain a healthy scepticism of our own.

16

Theories of the sexual division of labour

In 1985 in Canberra I resumed research on a book on women and work in Australia since 1945. I have since published several articles from the research done then. One of these was a survey of the literature on the twin problems of why women become housewives, and why when they do enter paid work it is generally into 'female' jobs. It was published the following year in a collection of essays, Australian Women: New Feminist Perspectives, *edited by Norma Grieve and Ailsa Burns.*

1985

Men and women are not dispersed throughout the labour market evenly; most occupations and many industries are either predominantly male or predominantly female. Within occupations and firms there is a further segregation between men's work and women's work, e.g. in retailing, in process work, in teaching. Since about 1970 a vast literature attempting to describe, measure, and explain this phenomenon has emerged. In many ways it is unsatisfactory. Not only are there serious problems in conceptualisation and measurement, but there has also been remarkably little progress in attempts to explain why such segregation—or as some would prefer to call it, 'concentration', to avoid certain pejorative implications—exists and persists.[1] Ruth Milkman has commented that 'an adequate theoretical account of the continuous reproduction of job segregation by sex in capitalist societies has yet to be developed'.[2] A 1984 OECD report on the subject concluded, after surveying the literature, that 'none of these economic approaches seems able to account for the level of persistence of this type of segregation'.[3] And Cynthia Lloyd and Beth Niemi, in their extended discussion, express a feeling of theoretical defeat: 'uncertainty as to the direction of causation becomes painfully evident'.[4]

The failure of explanation is evident in the Australian literature. One example is the work of Margaret Power, one of the most respected writers in the field. In 1985, with three co-workers, she wrote a long discussion of women and employment, as a submission to the Committee of Enquiry into Labour Market Programs.[5] In this paper, Power et al enumerate a list of causes of workforce segregation, including: employers' desire to divide and rule workers; male workers' desire and ability to keep good jobs for themselves; cultural sexism leading to women's greater responsibilities for domestic labour, which in turn limits many women to part-time work and therefore a limited range of occupations; women's exclusion from certain occupations via protective industrial legislation; channelling of girls and boys into the acquisition of different skills by educational authorities; and the apprenticeship system which has excluded women from many skilled trades. But these causes are simply added together—they do not specify in a theoretical sense the possible relationship between them.

This problem in explanation has consequences not only for theory. As D. Lewis put it in 1982: 'There is no consensus concerning the causes of the rise and persistence of sexual segregation in the labour force . . . Until . . . a consensus begins to emerge it will be difficult for governments to initiate programs to substantially lessen segregation.'[6] Government programs do indeed rest on theoretical assumptions about causation. Affirmative action programs generally rest on the notion that hiring and promotion practices are primarily responsible. Yet in so far as these programs include assertiveness training for women, they may also rest on an explanation emphasising female aspirations and skills; similarly, emphasis within these programs on techniques for dealing with male worker exclusivity implies that the latter is considered an important factor. Education and training programs, stressing non-traditional education for boys and girls, by implication lay stress on sex-role socialisation and the way this affects employment aspirations and usable skills. It would seem, then, worthwhile, from a policy as well as a theoretical point of view, to try and disentangle— and relate—the various elements supposed to contribute to job segregation. I undertake this task here through a review of some of the major theories and approaches to the problem of explaining how sexual divisions in the labour market arise.

Biological differences

A possible argument is that men and women do different kinds of jobs because they have different biologically based capacities. In this view, each sex does the work for which it is biologically suited. Men do the heavy work, women the work requiring manual dexterity.

The basic feminist point of the early 1970s at least—later feminism has returned enthusiastically to the notion of biological difference, at least in some versions—was that these differences are by and large nonexistent, that they are seen as differences only through a framework constituted by sexist ideology.[7] Most writers in the field today would accept the feminist critique in most cases, or at least would accept that very little of the occupational segregation observed can be attributed to these kinds of differences. Even writers with quite anti-feminist leanings accept that the degree of occupational segregation is far greater than biological differences would indicate. A very small proportion of jobs, for example, in a modern industrial economy depends on great muscular strength, and even those that do will be too onerous for some men, and not onerous for some women. In any case, cross-cultural comparisons and historical knowledge show us that women have worked at far more arduous jobs in other societies than allowed to do in this one. And the example of manual dexterity has been generally regarded as a justification of, rather than a reason for, the use of women on repetitive process work.

Inherited ideologies

There is a range of approaches that explains job segregation as a product of ideology rather than biology. These argue that jobs are segregated because of socially constructed beliefs that certain jobs are appropriate for males and others for females. How do these beliefs come about? One answer is that they are inherited from earlier historical periods, and simply taken over by industrial capitalism from the pre-industrial era. This was the view of earlier feminist theory: that is, women carry out in the labour market the kinds of activities they formerly did within the domestic economy—making clothing, food processing, preparation and serving, caring services such as nursing, and so on. In this view industrialisation may have changed quite profoundly the nature of the tasks required to produce goods and services, and the social relations entered into in the course of that production, but it has not altered the sex of the people who undertake those tasks.

This is the view that most people have in mind when referring to a 'sexual division of labour'. There is seen to be a single principle at

work, operating first *within* household production and then transferred holus-bolus to the marketplace. It is a view with some
validity, but cannot be pushed too far. While it is often true that
women are employed in industry to produce goods and services
similar to those produced in the domestic economy, it is not true
consistently.[8] Many occupations and industries have little or no
pre-industrial equivalent, e.g. secretarial work, administration,
while some economic activities such as spinning, weaving and
healing, when transferred from household to marketplace, actually
change their sex in the process.[9] In any case, to the degree that it is
true that pre-industrial divisions are transferred into industrial
production, we are still left to wonder why this might be so.

Socialisation

Some would explain this historical continuity as a product of
socialisation. The beliefs about certain kinds of work being 'male'
and others 'female' are values that are transmitted from generation
to generation. Boys and girls are trained differently, both at home
and at school, and thus acquire different skills, and seek and are
offered different jobs. A good example of this approach is Margaret
Power's 1975 article entitled 'The Making of a Woman's Occupation'.[10] Power stressed the very high degree of sex segregation in
the Australian labour market, and the fact that it was not significantly declining. She located the reasons for this situation largely in
the power of sex-role socialisation and sexist ideology, in keeping
with feminist arguments at that point: 'Different patterns of child
rearing and schooling create in men and women different person-
alities and aspirations, both of which affect their choice of, and
suitability for, different occupations.'

Particular attention has been paid by many writers to the ways in
which the education system produces school-leavers with very
different skills and aspirations according to gender. This literature
is reviewed quite extensively by Eileen Byrne who outlines its
debates on issues such as parental and school influence, teacher
sexism, and the role of careers counsellors.[11] It does point to
important processes, whereby differences in male and female
aspirations and skills are created and maintained. But it is
impossible to assess the importance of differential socialisation
until we have looked more closely at the social structure within
which it is embedded. As Eileen Byrne has suggested, girls'
aspirations and self-image are as likely to be formed by a realistic
appraisal of what lies ahead as by the actions of parents in the home
or teachers and peers at school.[12] And the socialisation thesis is
unable to explain change, such as the cases of jobs switching their
sex to which Margaret Power drew our attention.

Human capital theory

So far, this discussion has proceeded with little reference to the effect of the most important sexual division of all—the duality in human reproduction, and the caring and domestic activities that surround it. One approach which tries to show how the association of women rather than men with childcare influences the types of jobs men and women enter is human capital theory. Theorists in this school, such as Mincer and Polachek, begin by pointing out that while men expect continuous employment, women—because of their reproductive role—expect intermittent employment.[13] Men will therefore be more likely to undergo lengthy training in order to gain entry to high-paying jobs, while women will see such training as useless and will seek immediate employment. Men's and women's differential expectations, leading to differential acquisition of skills, will necessarily be realised since women's earning capacity is lower and therefore a period of workforce withdrawal not so drastic. As Lloyd and Niemi put it, a 'vicious circle' arises, but the starting point is regarded as women's realistic expectations of workforce intermittency.

A major problem with this approach is that it emphasises different *lengths* rather than different *types* of education. Yet gender differences in the former are no longer significant; differences in length of education are nowadays related far more closely to class than to gender. Job training continues its long-term shift from the workplace to specific educational institutions, nursing providing a recent example, and journalism another almost as recent. Within the education system, class takes over from gender as a basis for access to training, though gender remains an important determinant of *which* training. Since World War II there has been a largescale entry by middle-class females into the education system, a group which is then confronted by a sex discriminatory labour market. I would argue that this is one of the prime movers of feminism, for middle-class women are confronted with a basic social contradiction: society *apparently* rewards education with job opportunities and high wages, yet severely restricts these rewards for women.

Nevertheless, it is true—as human capital theorists point out—that men are concentrated in certain types of jobs and women in other types of jobs. But to understand how and why this is so, we need to move away, at least temporarily, from a focus on the socially created differences between men and women to a focus on how and why it is that there are differences in jobs at all.

Labour market segmentation

A very influential body of theory has been that of 'labour market segmentation'. This theory arose in the 1960s from Doeringer and

Piore's notion of 'internal labour markets'.[14] These develop, they argued, when workers attain skills on the job, and rise up a career ladder within one firm or organisation. Workers are tied to the firm if they wish to maintain their wage levels and advancement opportunities, and so the only decisive competition for jobs takes place at the point of entry. Internal labour markets rest on some identity of interest between employers and workers: employers value worker stability and low labour turnover, while the workers, or more precisely unions, seek protected jobs and career-ladder guarantees based on seniority. Later theorists argued that, if we consider all these internal labour markets together, we have, in a larger sense a 'primary labour market'—a set of jobs marked by security, good pay, and a career ladder.

But only some industries, firms or sections of firms work in this way. Others rely on labour which needs little on-the-job training. Their priority is to keep wages down, and worker loyalty and stability is not sought. These firms or industries provide jobs which form what is called a 'secondary labour market'. The distinction into primary and secondary labour markets, then, is the basis of what has become generally known as 'dual labour market theory'.[15] Later commentators have regarded the primary/secondary distinction as too simple and have started to argue for three or four segments—hence the shift in terminology to 'segmentation' theory. Richard Edwards, for example, in his book *Contested Terrain*, defines three segments: secondary, subordinate primary, and independent primary.[16] And Richard Kreckel explores proposals for both three- and fourfold divisions.[17]

These theorists explain labour market segmentation by employers' needs for low labour turnover and high job commitment for certain types of jobs, and for low wages and high turnover for other kinds. A more marxist inflection to the theory was provided by Edwards, Reich and Gordon, who emphasised issues not so much of direct efficiency as of an indirectly achieved efficiency via employer control of the labour process.[18] To counter working-class unity and militancy, they suggest, 'employers turned to strategies designed to divide and conquer the work force'. The large firms 'aimed to divide the labour force into various segments so that the actual experiences of workers would be different and the basis of their common opposition to capitalism would be undermined'.[19]

The theory has been used to explain why it is that not only do jobs differ from one another in these ways, but also different kinds of people seem to get different kinds of jobs. Why do certain ethnic groups within a working population seem to be employed only in particular kinds of jobs or particular industries? Why are some jobs filled by women and others by men? In 1976 two articles, one by R. D. Barron and B. M. Norris in the UK, and the other by Francine Blau and Carol Jusenius in the US, drew attention to the possibilities of the emerging dual or segmented labour market theory for the problem of occupational segregation by sex.[20] Both sets of authors pointed to the fact that the primary labour market was filled predominantly by men and the secondary labour market contained the mass of female workers. And many writers subsequently have made a similar point.

This idea has proved to be a useful conceptual tool when applied to a specific industry, for example in Desley Deacon's work on the emergence of a dual labour market in the New South Wales public service.[21] It is sometimes argued that the dual labour market theory holds that there are two non-competing labour markets for jobs, and individuals cannot cross from one to the other. Desley Deacon uses this idea to effect to describe the Commonwealth Public Service from 1901 to the late 1930s, where men and women were both formally and informally confined to quite different sets of jobs. Women could not reach authority positions, and had no career ladder. To explain why this is so Deacon turns to other theories; yet the notion of a dual labour market has given her a useful descriptive device.

Segmentation theory is useful more for its descriptive than for its explanatory power. One problem with it is that it cannot be used to explain why there is job segregation by sex *within* both the primary and the secondary sectors. Another is that within the theory itself, all kinds of explanations for job segregation by sex are advanced. Some writers, e.g. Barron and Norris, give reasons similar to those of the human capital theorists—women, because of workforce intermittency, do not achieve the training required for the primary labour market. Others, mainly those in a more marxist tradition, stress employer initiative in using worker sexism to their own ends in an overall strategy of divide and rule. The main Australian example of this approach lies in the work of Jock Collins who in 1977 and 1978 attempted to apply radical segmentation theory to Australia.[22] His argument was that the dispersal of men mainly into primary labour market jobs and women into secondary jobs is functional to capitalism, by providing 'the material basis for dividing the working class and creating low-wage manual segments dominated by migrant and female workers'. Thus it is employer control, rather than worker preference, that assigns men and women to different jobs, and this employer control exploits worker sexism for its own ends, through mechanisms which remain unclear.

Employer discrimination

Many economists argue that employer discrimination is based not on a cynical exploitation of worker sexism but rather on a belief that it is economically unwise to hire women for primary jobs.[23] That is, because most women will leave their job earlier than men will, or are at least thought to do so, then no woman will be hired for particular jobs. Thus employers stream men and women into the primary and secondary labour markets respectively.

It can be argued that it is rational for primary labour market employers to refuse to employ women, as they will usually not stay long enough to warrant the on-the-job training costs. But it may be that women are not in fact more likely to leave jobs than men are. Some researchers do argue that while women voluntarily leave the workforce altogether more frequently than men do, men are equally likely (for a variety of reasons) as women to leave a particular job. Bruce Chapman argues that women's apparently higher quit rates are related mainly to their greater concentration in low-wage—one could say secondary—jobs.[24] And the Office of the Status of Women has argued that women's quit rates in a given firm or occupation are no higher, indeed may even be lower, than those of men. Thus employer discrimination is seen to be based on an inaccurate assessment of male and female labour market behaviour. D. Lewis has shown in one study that a group of Australian employers systematically overestimated women's quit rates relative to men's.[25]

This research is useful in revealing the extent to which job behaviour is determined by the job as much as the sex of the worker. Yet it may be unwise to hinge too much policy on an argument that there is no difference in quit rates. The fact is that women do have a reason for leaving jobs that men do not generally have—i.e. childbearing. Maternity leave measures are meant to help deal with this gender-based difference, assisting both employers (in that they need not lose skilled workers) and women workers themselves. Such measures are probably applicable mainly to primary jobs, and have their problems, but they do remind us that men and women do not enter, or leave, the labour market on exactly the same basis.

Thus, while radical segmentation theory attributes job segregation to cynical employer manipulation of sexual antagonism, discrimination theories attribute it to inadequate information. Neither of these approaches appears entirely satisfactory, one attributing to employers a lack of immediate concern with profitability, and the other a level of inefficiency that is difficult to accept. One must assume that employers are out to maximise profits, and that if they discriminate between men and women as thoroughly as they do, then within this framework of profit maximisation, they have good reason to do so.

Male workers and industrial organisation

The search for reasons has led some theorists to emphasise the pressures successfully exerted by organised male workers as the source of job segregation. Their role has been a subject of debate among both marxists and feminists, and underlying the debate is another about the relationship between class and gender, theoretically and politically.

One issue under discussion is the role of the working class— rather than employers—in establishing a system where married women were largely excluded from the labour market, and single women were excluded from the male trades and occupations. The question of the protection of 'male jobs' very often becomes in this debate inseparable from that of sex-based wage differences. It is an argument about how it was that male wages, at least for skilled and semi-skilled workers, came to reach a level sufficient to support a family, while female wages were generally barely sufficient to support the female worker herself.

In the second half of the nineteenth century, male wages sufficient to support a full-time housewife as well as children came to be called a 'family wage'. The concept of a family wage was common in industrial societies; in Australia it was formalised within the arbitration system through Judge Higgins' 'Harvester judgment' of 1907, and the 'Mildura Fruit Pickers' judgment'—in effect a female basic wage case—of 1912. It is generally agreed that the family wage was secured at least in part as the result of male trade union action. Disagreement arises over whether this action should be interpreted as representing the desires and wishes of the working class as a whole, or of only its male members.

The champion of the former case has been Jane Humphries, who argued in 1977 that the working class in the nineteenth century fought hard for a situation where a working-class housewife would not have to enter the labour market, in preference to one where all family members had to work, rendering labour oversupplied and cheap.[26] This aim could be realised only by keeping out of the skilled and semi-skilled manual trades workers who were unskilled and/or likely to accept a lower rate of pay, which often meant women. The material foundation of the antagonism between the unions and women workers was women's cheapness, and their use by employers as unskilled labour after new machinery had been introduced. While exclusive policies worked against the possibility of achieving equal pay, they did prevent employers from using female labour to undermine the position of male workers in the skilled trades.

Humphries is arguing that the defence of male trades was, in the environment of nineteenth-century industrial capitalism, a defence of the family. Like Michael Anderson, she sees the family as the means whereby the newly created working class coped with the enormous strains placed upon it by the new economic system. Kin helped each other deal with crises. As capitalist relations of production expanded, the proletarianisation of some family members was essential, since the productivity of wage labour rose relative to that of domestic work and self-support in agriculture was no longer possible. But not all members entered wage labour, since there was insufficient demand for it, and not all, e.g. the old or very young, could work. The working class furthermore hated various forms of charitable and state support, especially as they often, for example in the case of workhouses, separated families. It preferred to keep its own support system, in the face of the increasing insecurity engendered by wage dependence. This support system was enhanced by the family wage and the full-time housewife. (In Australia, a similar case has been argued—with little Australian detail—by Theresa Brennan.[27])

This kind of argument was subject to the feminist criticism that it saw the family as a decision-making unit rather than an arena wherein men control women. It was seen as ignoring the powerful influence of sexist ideology, and of sexual policies and dynamics. The alternative account was initiated in Heidi Hartmann's 1976 article 'Capitalism, Patriarchy, and Job Segregation by Sex'.[28] Hartmann's argument was similar to that of Humphries except that she saw the exclusion of women from male trades as dictated not by the interests and actions of the working class, or at least the better-off sections of it, but by the interests and actions of men against women. The maintenance of women's domestic labour through the single-income ('family wage') family is interpreted not as a working-*class* strategy for survival but as an exploitation of working-class *women* by working-class men. Hartmann, then, stresses working-class male sexism as a key to segmentation. Employers adapted to male worker exclusivism, and also were constrained by protective legislation. In Hartmann's view, this legislation, which excluded women either directly or indirectly from certain trades, was also a product of male worker sexism.

Somewhere between Humphries and Hartmann lies the work of Ruth Milkman, who has studied the role of unions in American history in excluding women from the male trades.[29] She argues that this role was very significant, and that this exclusion was one of the reasons that it was the service sector that women entered in large numbers during the twentieth century. She also, however, argues that the fear of women undercutting men in the labour market could logically lead either to exclusion or inclusion (we must organise the women if they are not to undercut us), and that in fact different sections of the American labour movement have historically adopted differing tactics. It is the craft unions that have led the drive to exclude women.

Hartmann's argument has been extraordinarily influential in marxist feminist accounts, for example that by Barrett and

McIntosh, which increasingly attribute married women's exclusion from the workforce and single women's exclusion from male trades to the sexist actions of male workers.[30] One example in Australia is the argument by Claire Williams in *Open Cut*.[31] She suggests that this is seen in its most extreme form in union-dominated mining towns like Mount Isa. In such towns there are few traditionally female jobs, and unionists work tirelessly to ensure that married women are sacked in favour of single women, and the single women are kept out of men's work. Williams, like Hartmann, attributes this to a sexist desire for women's labour in the home.

Johanna Brenner and Maria Ramas in 1984 launched a critique of the increasingly popular Hartmann line, returning to Humphries' notion of working-*class* defence of the family wage rather than *male* insistence upon it as a means of controlling the labour of women.[32] They point out that in the nineteenth and twentieth centuries the entry of women into a trade did indeed depress the wages it could command, by increasing the labour supply, undermining claims of skill, and supplying less industrially aggressive workers. They also examine more closely than Jane Humphries had done the problem of why it was women rather than men whose labour was to be used for childcare, the achievement of domestic comfort, and family survival. Women rather than men did the childcaring, they argued, because their biological involvement in pregnancy, childbearing, and lactation made them the logical candidates for this role. Since childcaring could not be undertaken in the new industrial work-places and the state would not provide facilities such as childcare, working-class families were forced to withdraw women from the labour market for a period. Similar constraints, they say, operate today, though much less severely. There is still not adequate commercial or state provision of support services such as childcare to release all married women for full-time waged labour.

Their argument is close to my own, advanced in 1981.[33] There I argued that since it was necessary in working-class families for women's relation to waged labour to be intermittent, it was important to guarantee the male wage. Since women could command only a low wage, they had to be excluded from men's work. My main difference from the later Brenner/Ramas argument lies in the explanation of why it is women, not men, who are the childcarers and domestic workers. They attribute this basically to the poor fit between biological reproduction and early industrial capitalist production, while I attributed it to ideology, to social beliefs that this was right and proper. Their emphasis on the importance of biology—of pregnancy, childbearing, and lactation—is valid, but it is hard to conceive of biological 'necessity' devoid of ideological content and cultural tradition.

Arguments about how it was that a 'family wage' came to be

payable to skilled and semi-skilled male workers have a particular twist in Australia, owing to our distinctive system of wage-fixing via centralised arbitration institutions. Edna Ryan and Anne Conlon's *Gentle Invaders* has been most influential in developing a specifically Australian account.[34] Like Hartmann, Ryan and Conlon attribute the family wage, and the consequent segregation of male and female trades, to sexist ideology, but in their case the sexism is not so much that of the unions as of the arbitration courts. They show how the arbitration courts developed the concept of the family wage as an ideological basis for unequal pay from the turn of the century until 1972.

Laura Bennett has described this position as a simple form of cultural determinism, where legal, economic and political structures simply reflect cultural definitions of women's role.[35] Ryan and Conlon, she says, focus far too much on the court's explicitly sexist pronouncements, and do not see how it operated under 'specific economic and political constraints'. Thus they attribute a differential basic wage to the court's—sometimes simply Higgins' own individual—sexist ideology. Bennett points out that the court rarely departed in its early days from existing wage rates. Its decision setting women's wage rates at 54 per cent of the male rate was close to the rate previously achieved, for example in the clothing trades, before their first award. The court's wage-setting criteria were not primarily ideological, but economic and political. The court's legitimacy depended on its not straying too far from existing practice. As a result the practice of recognising jobs as male or female and setting wage rates accordingly was a political necessity.

Claiming skill

The argument thus far rests on the view that men have been successful in excluding women from the primary jobs—the skilled, secure, high-paying jobs. But recent debate questions the assumption that these jobs really do involve more skill than secondary jobs. Perhaps they are simply *seen* as more skilled. Are the trades that men occupy really more skilled than those women fill, or is it simply that male workers have been more effective in *claiming* skill, and payment for it?

One strand of argument stresses that *perceptions* of skill are sex-linked. What women do will be perceived by employers and arbitrators to be less skilled than what men do. Anne Phillips and Barbara Taylor follow Harry Braverman in arguing that deskilling is occurring but that skill labels in some cases have been maintained.[36] Braverman argues that the trend in modern industry is to large-scale deskilling, resulting from a combination of new technologies, and employers' desire to control the labour process ever more closely. Workers attempt to prevent this deskilling through opposition to the new technologies and to work reorganisation, but generally they fail to achieve this goal. Nevertheless, some groups of workers are able to insist that their work is not in fact now low-skill, and these will generally be male workers. Phillips and Taylor regard men's more successful assertion of skill as motivated by a desire to 'retain their dominance within the sexual hierarchy'; they see male worker action as an attack on women rather than as a defence against employers. Very much in the same tradition is the work of Cynthia Cockburn, who in her well-known book *Brothers* has argued that in the printing industry male workers were able to have their semi-skilled work defined as skilled, and were motivated by sexist ideology in excluding women from the trade.[37]

The emphasis in this kind of work, then, is on worker sexism. But one could put the case for the role of union organisation in job differentiation without arguing that male workers are motivated by ideas about women's place being in the home, by selfish desires to retain women's labour there, or by sexual stereotypes about what constitutes proper work for women or men. The role of unions can be seen as a defensive one against capitalist power and deskilling. The desire to maximise return for labour leads unions to pursue strategies in the workplace that effectively exclude women.

In an influential article called 'Structured Labour Markets, Worker Organisation and Low Pay', Jill Rubery criticised both dual and radical theories of labour market segmentation for their emphasis on the actions of employers, and their lack of attention to worker strategies.[38] Workers will seek to maximise the return on their labour, and their most effective strategies for doing so, she argued, will be to control entry to an occupation, firm, or industry and to assert that group's irreplaceable skills, via apprenticeships and seniority rules. If it can assert its non-replaceability in this way, its bargaining power against management is enhanced. The need to control entry will lead organised workers to exclude new labour sources, typically women or immigrants.

In Australia, Carol O'Donnell, in *The Basis of the Bargain*, has also argued that control of entry has proved important both in defending wage levels and excluding women.[39] As she puts it, 'men have been more industrially active than women in defining the work/education relationship in a way which suits their industrial interests'. They have been able to a greater degree to defend wage levels through the assertion of skill, and thus the necessity for training. In particular the skilled unions have been able in some cases to insist on unnecessarily long apprenticeships. Laura Bennett in 'The Construction of Skill' also sees ability to insist on length of training as crucial to ability to claim skill.[40] Both employers and employees, she argues, have had a common interest in artificially extending apprenticeships—the former to use apprentices as cheap labour in the short term, the employees to gain a basis for skill assertion in the long term. There were few apprenticeships in female trades because women lacked the political strength to insist upon it.

O'Donnell interprets men's greater success in claiming skill as the product of their superior industrial organisation and strength. She sees current job segregation as a product of a history of technological innovation, and workers' industrial responses to it. Where new technologies tend to deskill, male workers insist that deskilling has not occurred.[41] In fact they are often successful in asserting that the opposite has happened, that the new technology requires greater skill. And the hostility of the worker to the machine is circumvented by the raising of pay, for those workers sufficiently organised to secure this pay-off. These workers tend to be men. Further, the huge number of classifications in male areas is the result of this ability to assert skill, to 'forge job classifications which represent differences in pay, conditions, and status. What exists is not so much a wide variety of jobs, as a history of industrial development and struggle.'

Bennett is even more radical than Rubery and O'Donnell in her rejection of an objectively definable level of skill. She argues it is not enough to point out that trade union power will affect definitions and recognitions of skill. We can see other influences at work when we examine the proceedings of the Australian Conciliation and Arbitration Court, which render visible many of the processes that are elsewhere obscured by the closed nature of collective bargaining. These proceedings show that court acceptance of skill was based on the *width* of the range of tasks required, rather than on difficulty per se, since assessment of task *difficulty* would have been near impossible. So the more tasks an occupation could encompass, the stronger the position of that group of workers in claiming skill. A union's ability to monopolise a wide range of skills for its members, however, was dependent not only on its industrial strength but also on the economic character of that industry, i.e. on the degree to which it suited employers to retain broadly rather than narrowly trained workers. Conversely, women's work in industry was defined and rewarded as unskilled not only because women workers lacked the power necessary to mount craft-type industrial organisations, but also because the industries in which they worked were economically conducive to fragmentation rather than to the maintenance of a broad coherence of tasks. Industries with the technological capacity to divide work were more likely to employ female labour, since it was cheap and more docile before technological change. And industries reliant on female labour were likely to take advantage of its cheapness and high turnover, by developing very high task fragmentation, as in clothing.

Bennett's work is interesting in questioning the equivalence between fragmentation and deskilling assumed in Braverman and in post-Braverman analyses, on the basis that the notion that skill means a range of tasks is an ideological and not a natural one. She also develops the point made by Rubery and O'Donnell that the reasons the craft unions worked hard to keep new tasks within the exclusive province of the craft worker were not primarily to do with sexism but because women's 'cheap unorganised labour was a threat to the craft unions' monopoly over certain kinds of work'. Her project is to develop explanations that rely as little as possible on either sexist ideology or on domestic divisions. I don't think she entirely succeeds, for in the end, in explaining why women's labour was fragmented and why male workers feared them as cheap workers, she necessarily relies on women's initial cheapness and intermittency as final explanations. Yet the value of her work lies in its much more detailed, elaborated, and complex discussion of the notion of skill than is usual. She shows also that Australian work on the issue can have special advantages, so far unutilised, because of the unusually explicit nature of negotiation on these issues via the arbitration system.

At the other end of the scale from Bennett is the work of Ann Game and Rosemary Pringle. Their book *Gender at Work* appeared in 1983 and has been very influential.[42] While they do agree that the greater recognition of male work as skilled derives largely from 'trade union struggles to maintain the definition of jobs as skilled in order to preserve male wage rates' (p. 18), the emphasis in their analysis is not on why and how a sexual division of labour is constructed, but on its ideological and industrial effects. They are concerned with the ways in which 'masculinity and femininity are produced in *relation* to each other through work' on the one hand, and how changes in the labour process are 'obscured by the sexual division of labour' (p. 23) on the other. Thus their account of how work is sexually segregated is generally descriptive rather than explanatory. They outline several axes along which men's and women's work might be differentiated within the one plant or industry or office: skilled/unskilled, heavy/light, dangerous/safe, dirty/clean, interesting/boring, and mobile/immobile. One of their main concerns is to investigate how technological change affects the sexual division of labour in a given industry. They show how new automated machinery can lead either to masculinisation, as in the whitegoods industry, or to feminisation, as in banking and retailing, of the workforce, but do not explain why a sexual division of labour exists, or why technological change has these diverse effects. In rejecting or modifying various theories such as that derived from Braverman which equates deskilling and feminisation, they appear to reject the theoretical quest altogether.

Conclusion

From this survey, it is clear that sexual division in the labour market arises from an interaction between bio-cultural tradition and practices on the one hand, and the specific institutions of capitalist production on the other. In this concluding section I attempt to specify the nature of this interaction more precisely.

First, a capitalist economy structures not only distinctive productive relations, but also a distinctive kind of family-household. That is, economic support is gained through either capital or wages, but only part of the population is in a direct wage relationship as employer or employee. Others may engage in all kinds of subsistence activities, but by and large as the market expands, dependence is created for those who are not directly within it. This dependence is generally mediated via either the state or kinship obligations, or both. That is, within an industrial capitalist economy there is an incomplete proletarianisation of the non-owning population.

Second, the work of personal caring remains largely within the household. Childcaring, for example, has not been fully commercialised or taken over by the state. There is still a great deal of it that occurs on a private level, affected but not incorporated by capitalist relations of production. This private caring is sustained through dependence on a wage earner, or an owner of capital.

Third, this private caring activity is done largely by women, for reasons of biological logic and cultural tradition. While men *can* care and nurture as well as women, it is rare that they choose or are forced to do so.

Fourth, given this bio-cultural connection of women to human reproductive activities, and given the continuation of private domestic labour including especially childcaring, men and women relate to the labour market differently. Women's participation in it is lower. During the nineteenth century, married women were withdrawn from the labour market if at all possible, as a means of ensuring adequate care of children, provision of domestic comforts, and crisis caring within kinship units.

Fifth, women's lower participation rates meant, historically, that when they *were* in the labour market, they commanded less remuneration than men. They lacked the power necessary to organise industrially on a craft basis. As a result female labour was sought by employers as a means of undercutting the existing male rates. Industries (or firms or parts of firms) with—or in the process of acquiring—the technological capacity to divide work were more likely to employ female labour. Once they were reliant on such labour, they could further develop high task fragmentation.

Sixth, employers' ability to pay women workers low wages led male unions to campaign for the exclusion of women from the male trades. The desire for and achievement by skilled and semi-skilled male workers of a family wage, together with the inability of women to command such a wage, thus laid a basis for job segregation by sex. Without the wage differential, a great many jobs that were male or female, when initially created *as* jobs within industrial capitalist relations of production, would more easily have become mixed-sex occupations as time went on.

Seventh, once it is the case that men earn more than women— still the case today—then a material as well as an ideological base is laid for women rather than men continuing to withdraw from the labour force for a period for childcaring purposes. And so the cycle is perpetuated. To the extent that childcare is continually socialised, the gap between men's and women's employment rates will continue to close. Economic conditions or political and cultural forces, however, may keep women in the increasingly unproductive household.

Eighth, the protection of the family wage in the male trades was often expressed in terms of what was proper work for men and women, and such notions derived also from the pre-industrial model. In some cases, biologically based differences in muscular strength played a role in allocating certain jobs to men. These notions and precedents helped determine which jobs would be male and which female, but not the fact of job segregation itself.

Ninth, once a job was firmly entrenched as male or female, only people of the sex seen as appropriate for that job were trained to do it. This restricted supply further reinforced perception of the job as male or female.

Tenth, job segregation by sex is likely to be undermined by several developments—women's growing employment rates, the closing of the gap between male and female wage rates and also between male and female years of education, and the political impetus of feminism. Job shortage, however, is a barrier to change.

Eleventh, and finally, the division between men and women in the labour market—in terms of amount, type of, and returns for participation—is the product of a fundamental contradiction between the continuation of a family-household structure and capitalist relations of production. The sexual division of labour we observe, and the sexist ideologies in which we live, register this contradiction.

17

The return to biology

In the schematic conclusion to the preceding chapter, my third point had been that women cared for children 'for reasons of biological logic and cultural tradition'. In this suggestion that sexual biological difference could and did have social consequences, I had (along with many others) reversed my earlier position, which had denied this was possible. This was a worldwide, though not universal, trend in feminism, ably documented by Hester Eisenstein in her book Contemporary Feminist Thought. [1] *An influential contribution to the Australian debate was Moira Gatens' article 'A critique of the sex/gender distinction' in 1984, which criticised earlier feminist attempts to eliminate the significance of the body in social life.[2] I wrote the following unpublished article in 1985.*

1985

Why is most childcaring done by women?

A major theoretical question for any study of women's work must be: why is it largely women who care for children and do housework, not only in Australia, but also, it seems, everywhere? For many this is a non-question, for it is seen as self-evident that women do these things because it is natural and proper that they do. They bear the children, they care for them. Frequently, a religious answer may be given: it is God's will that women care for children, the family, and the home, and that men provide for this family. But for sociologists and historians the answer cannot be so simple. Why and how is a biological difference translated into a social difference? This is one of the oldest questions for social science, and underlies one of its oldest debates—often known as 'nature versus nurture'. How important are matters of inherited intelligence and temperament compared with those resulting from socialisation and social organisation? The debate has flared in such areas as 'race and intelligence' and in educational policy; it is particularly bitter and pertinent in debates over the rights and duties of women and men.

In an article entitled 'Theorising Gender', Bob Connell, sociologist and pro-feminist, has restated the commonly argued case that social differences cannot be explained by biological ones. 'There must be first,' he says, 'a really thorough rejection of the notion that natural difference is a "basis" of gender, that the social patterns are somehow an "elaboration" of natural difference.' [3] For Connell, the social cannot follow from the natural. The social is, almost by definition, 'radically unnatural'. He argues that biology is relevant to but does not in any way determine, social structures; and that social processes deal with, but are not in any way whatsoever determined by, the biological patterns given to them.

This was the position of feminism in the early 1970s, and still is of some strands within feminism today. Janet Sayers, a British feminist psychologist, calls it 'social constructionism'. [4] It asserts that since the observable differences between men and women are socially, not biologically, based, they are subject to change and human volition. Men and women can live on the basis of equality, and biological difference should not be seen as a justification for inequality. This kind of feminism then goes on to argue, as does Connell, that biological difference has no relevance for the understanding of social life. As Penelope Brown and L. Jordanova put it in 1981, 'what cultures make of sex differences is almost infinitely variable, so that biology cannot be playing a determining role. Men and women are products of social relations . . .'. [5]

It would follow, then, that women's association with childcaring has nothing to do with the fact that they, and not men, give birth to children. The explanation for the association has to be sought elsewhere, in the realm of the social. Yet there have been very few attempts indeed to provide such an account. Even Talcott Parsons, who provides a thoroughly social account of the nuclear family stressing its peculiar ability to serve certain essential social functions—securing the emotional balance of adults, and the socialisation of children—reverts to biology when considering the reasons for the 'universal fact' that women are more intimately concerned with childcare than are men. 'Lactation,' he says, plays 'a very fundamental part.' [6] And for Margaret Mead, another whose name is generally associated with an emphasis on the very great differences in human behaviour across different societies, the mother–child association does not need explaining. What is more interesting for her is the problem of why men provide for women and children. Nurturing behaviour by men is learned, but women's nurturing of their own children is not: 'The mother's nurturing tie to her child is apparently so deeply rooted in the actual biological conditions of conception and gestation, birth and suckling, that only fairly complicated social arrangements can break it down entirely . . . Women may be said to be mothers unless they are taught to deny their childrearing qualities.' This 'desire to provide for a child they have already nourished for nine months within the safe circle of their own bodies' is natural, and only outside social forces can break it.[7]

Nor have feminist scholars been able to provide a social explanation for an association which seems to span all cultures and all historical periods. Among feminists more energy has been devoted to showing why there is no natural necessity for childcaring to be distributed unequally, for example in arguments against a 'maternal instinct', than to confronting the problem of just why it is indeed distributed unequally. There has, too, been more interest in the effects of, than the reasons for, the woman–childcare associ-ation. Ernestine Friedl's *Women and Men: An Anthropologist's View* is in this tradition as she asks, not 'why do women mother?', but rather how women adjust their childbearing patterns (e.g. spacing of children) and childrearing practices to their other social and economic activities.[8] Looking at the same issue the other way around, two writers whose names are most clearly associated with a feminist account of mothering, namely Nancy Chodorow and Dorothy Dinnerstein, do not ask why women were universally in charge of infant and early childcare but rather how that association affected women's social and economic position, and the psychic structures of human beings, both male and female.[9] Feminist explanations of the woman–childcare association have been viti-ated also by a confusion of this particular question with others— such as 'why are males dominant and females subordinate?', or 'why the family?'. This is clearly evident in Kate Millett, but also in many other writers. Within feminist theory, then, the focus on 'why do women mother?' has been surprisingly weak.

Ironically, one of the few serious attempts to tackle the issue came up with a biological-determinist answer. Shulamith Firestone, in *The Dialectics of Sex,* argued that 'sex class' sprang directly from a biological reality. Women care for children because they bear them. 'Nature produced the fundamental inequality—half the human race must bear and rear the children of all of them—which was later consolidated, institutionalised, in the interests of men.[10]

The implication is clear. If biology is indeed destiny, then the social reliance on that biology must be overcome; childbirth as we know it must be replaced by artificial human reproduction.

The body

It is not only in explaining why women mother that feminist theory has faced severe problems. The problem of the biological foundation (if any) of gender relationships at large has in fact become a very difficult one for feminist theory. Within American feminism, an initially anti-biological-determinist position was supplanted increasingly during the 1970s and 1980s by one which saw biological difference as a basis for social and psychic differences between men and women, as the starting point for sexual identity and character. And it was not only American radical feminism which returned to the idea of biological determination. French feminism, via rereadings of Freud, reasserted the importance of bodily (biological) difference for a sense of sexual identity, of being masculine or feminine. And this sense of identity, this imaginary body, was essential for understanding sexual difference. The interest within French feminism in psychic difference has led it away from Simone de Beauvoir's famous dictum in her 1949 work, *The Second Sex:* 'one is not born a woman, one becomes a woman.' Evelyne Sullerot, another French feminist, replies that 'one is indeed born a woman, with a physical destiny programmed differently from that of a man'.[11] Sullerot says, quite correctly, that modern feminism's original opposition to any hint of biological determination stemmed from the apparently inescapable conclusion that if biology is determinant in this way, then women have no control over their own destiny, cannot change the way society is organised. Feminists, she suggests, should abandon this fear of finding biological determinations, for the conclusion does not follow from the premise. Human beings can change what seems permanent and natural. Indeed, she argues,

> it seems to be much easier to change natural than cultural facts. It was much easier to relieve women from obligatory breastfeeding than to make fathers give babies their bottles. It is much easier to develop contraceptives that eliminate the menstrual cycle than to change women's attitude toward menstruation. It is inertia built into cultural phenomena that seems to slow down our control over natural phenomena.[12]

Sullerot appears to be quite typical of French feminism in asserting the continuing salience both of biological difference and existential freedom: 'one can change this [physical] destiny and become what one wants to be, one can comply with this destiny or deliberately move away from it.'[13]

Mia Campioni and Elizabeth Gross have argued in an Australian context for a French-influenced radical feminism. They called for a recognition of 'the role of the body in constituting consciousness'. Women's oppression, they suggest, can only be understood 'in terms of the existence of sexually differentiated bodies . . . The point is that we are not disembodied subjects, consciousnesses distinct from bodies'.[14] Yet Campioni and Gross are not very interested in asking sociological or historical questions, with the result that it is difficult to apply their perspectives to answering questions like 'why is it women who mother?'.

A different reassertion of the importance of biological difference was made by Janet Sayers in *Biological Politics*. She rejected both 'social constructionism' and 'biological essentialism'—the notion that men and women have distinct biologically based, masculine or feminine characteristics. Sayers called for a third, 'middle', position, on the grounds that where biological essentialism neglected social and historical sources of sexual difference, social constructionism 'underestimates its biological roots'.[15]

I would want to argue that we cannot use biological difference to justify social inequality, or even to justify the continuation of an association between women and childcaring that is greater than that between men and childcaring. On the other hand, I would also want to argue that in constructing an historical explanation of the woman–childcare association as it has existed and continues to exist, we must take full account of sex-based biological difference. When confronted with such a universal pattern, the only basis for universality does indeed lie in the body, in the fact that human reproduction relies on a biological duality between male and female. The only commonality we can be sure of, theoretically, is that in all societies this biological duality is given social meaning, is constituted as a basis for sexual division. Connell's radically anti-biology position is ultimately very hard to sustain; it seems impossible, in the end, to believe that women's association with childcaring has, historically, nothing to do with their role in giving birth and with lactation. It is equally hard to see how, in Connell's terms, a social process can 'deal with' anything and not be in some way affected by it. How can we conceive of social arrangements surrounding human reproduction which are blind to its biological duality? It should be possible to give sex-based biological difference a role in history, without allowing it to be seen as inescapable, and therefore a guideline, a prescription, for the future. It is not, however, necessary to give it a role conceptualised as distinct from that of social and historical determination. The strength and forms of sexual division will depend not on biological difference itself, but on the nature of the society in question, on its accumulated historical traditions, its mode of production, its political structure, and its ideological, religious, and cultural practices.

PART VI

Coming to terms with the colonial past

18

Colonial women's history

In 1984 Katrina Alford's book Production or Reproduction? An economic history of women in Australia 1788–1850, appeared.[1] After the rush of books in Australian women's history in 1975 there had been something of a lull in single-authored books on Australian women's history. There had been a lot of work done for the Women and Labour conferences of 1978, 1980, and 1982, each of which resulted in an essay collection on aspects of Australian women's history. There were other collections, too, such as Marilyn Lake and Farley Kelly's Double Time, Patricia Crawford's Exploring Women's Past, and a multi-edited collection entitled Families in Colonial Australia. As well, journal articles appeared in Hecate, and to a lesser extent in Labour History, Historical Studies and Refractory Girl. Now, in the mid-1980s, there was another rush of single-authored books, this time based largely on research originally undertaken for doctoral theses. As well as Alford's, there were, most notably, Jill Julius Matthews' Good and Mad Women: The historical construction of femininity in twentieth-century Australia, already briefly referred to in chapter 13, and Kerreen Reiger's The Disenchantment of the Home: Modernising the Australian Family 1880–1940.[2]

I reviewed Alford's book for the ABC, and the review was subsequently published in Hecate. I had never met Katrina Alford, and it was a critical review. In a small environment like Australian women's history, however, we were bound to meet sooner or later; when we did, in 1985, it was embarrassing for both of us. For whatever reason, I have not reviewed any Australian women's history since.

1984

A book on early colonial Australian women's history is timely on three counts. First, there is the remarkable growth of general public interest in Australian history, fuelled by a combination of a revived cultural nationalism, the approaching Bicentennial year in 1988, and the popularity of historical dramas evident in the expanding Australian film and television industries. Second, there is the special fascination of the convict period among popular audiences. Quite apart from a slightly pornographic interest in floggings and debauchery, prostitution, rape, and sodomy, there is the striking human drama of the period. Here we have the imposition on an unsuspecting Aboriginal people of an army of officials and prisoners from a geographically and culturally distant part of the world. Each side was at first curious about, and then horrified, by what it saw. Both wanted the same resource—the land itself. The ensuing conflicts between or within these groupings underlie the kind of society we live in today. And the third reason Alford's book is timely is that it is about women's history. As the ideas which germinated in the feminist ferment of the 1970s find expression in the 1980s in more and more books by and about women, an audience for women's history seems guaranteed.

So, on all these counts, I picked up Katrina Alford's *Production or Reproduction? An Economic History of Women in Australia 1788–1850* with interest. What would it add to our understanding of Australian history, of our early colonial history, and of women's history? Would it suggest new ways of understanding the dynamics of colonisation, the development of capitalism, the operations of the convict system, the emergence of class society, the property relations and organisation of work, the political conflicts of those first 62 years of the British invasion of this continent? Would it show that a focus on women's history suggests new ways of understanding Australian history as a whole?

The answer, sadly, has to be no. Alford's book captures little of the human drama of this period, and provides little of the hard economic analysis we need if her topic is to be understood. I'll return to the book's failings in a moment. But first, let's see what it actually does.

The central theme of Alford's book is the very narrow range of work options available to white colonial women. The politically and ideologically preferred option was marriage, an occupation in itself. Marriage was seen by the authorities and by the upper and middle classes as essential for social stability and morality, and women's tasks were to be, therefore, essentially childbearing and domestic work. But this ideal of marriage as the proper role and occupation for women had, Alford shows, different effects for women of different social classes. For upper-class women, marriage was really the only option, supplemented perhaps by philanthropy—good charitable works. For middle-class women, marriage was the main option, though there was some possibility of employment for single middle-class women as governesses and teachers. For free working-class women—ex-convicts, free immigrants, and those born in the colony—the main employment option other than marriage was domestic service and, to a lesser extent, agricultural labour. For convict women it seems that marriage did not constitute an alternative to employment, and they were set to work either in domestic service or in the Female Factories at Parramatta and Hobart where they were employed at laundry work, making clothing, and in wool and linen textile manufacture.

Alford explains this narrow range of occupations open to women as arising firstly from British notions about women as unsuited for heavy manual labour outside domestic service and secondly from the nature of the colonial economy where the main labour required was exactly for those heavy manual tasks regarded as unsuitable for women.

The second theme Alford explores is the extent of upper-class denunciation of working-class, especially convict, women on the grounds of their immorality, depravity, and sexual licentiousness. She shows the profound hypocrisy of these upper-class attacks on convict women's morality. The convicts, women and men, had been torn from their family context in Britain. By Alford's account one-quarter of them were forced to leave husbands or wives behind. They were segregated on the voyage out, but then were allowed to mix pretty freely on arrival. The restraints which had operated in Britain—reputation amongst family and friends and employers—were gone. The officer class often consorted and cohabited with the women freely and, further, the women were daily surrounded by womanless convict men. So strong was the employers' denunciation of convict women's sexual immorality that they were, according to Alford, often rejected as domestic servants even when these were needed and scarce.

In general, then, Alford argues that a combination of a pioneering rural economy and British-derived notions of women's proper economic and sexual role worked together to make the lives of white colonial women of all classes narrow and confined. Women of all classes were oppressed by the operations of sexist ideology in a colonial economy, and the main differences between them were that working-class women had to work much harder and for less material gain than did their middle- and upper-class sisters. As well, they carried the additional burden of being categorised, despised, and stigmatised as immoral.

All this sounds interesting enough. Why, then, did I find this book so disappointing?

First, Alford fails to place her analysis within the context of the process of colonisation itself. It is resolutely a white women's history, curiously devoid of any awareness that the situation facing these women was framed by the ongoing struggle to dispossess Aborigines of their land. Throughout the period she examines, Aboriginal societies were invaded, exploited, and in some cases destroyed by an incoming European population. This colonisation process not only had drastic effects for Aboriginal people but also laid the basis for the establishment of a particular kind of European society on this continent. White women entered rural areas either as wives or servants, usually after Aboriginal resistance had been quelled. Their sexual exploitation must be seen in the context of the widespread sexual exploitation of Aboriginal women.[3] Their economic exploitation must be seen as having been made possible by the dispossession and economic exploitation of Aboriginal people. Their use as domestic labour must be seen in the context of the degree to which Aboriginal labour was sought or avoided. And quite apart from all this, a book claiming to be about women in Australia in this early colonial period should have included Aboriginal women, since they were, for most of the period, the majority of the female population.

Second, as economic history this book is curiously limited. Nowhere is there an extended discussion of the changing nature of the colonial economy. We learn very little about the development of agriculture, sheep farming, cattle farming, the maritime industries, building and construction, trade and commerce. Most damaging of all, we learn little about domestic service, taken as an industry as a whole. We don't learn what level of domestic comfort was achieved by various classes in colonial society, how those levels changed over time, or the extent to which these services were provided by either wage labour or by women, and indeed men, within various social classes doing them for themselves. We learn nothing of the nature of domestic work itself, its level of technological development, or the property relations underlying it. We also hear little about childcare practices in different social classes, and how the labour of child-caring was provided. Indeed we learn little about the property relations in any of the colonial industries—the size of different kinds of enterprises, the proportion of small and large employers, the prevalence of wage labour, the processes of capital accumulation within the colonies and the importation of British capital. So it's a history written in a vacuum.

Without this kind of analysis it is difficult indeed to see how

Alford could explain why the sexual division of labour in the
colonies took the form it did. She appears at the very beginning to
avoid the task of explanation altogether, announcing on the first
page that 'the book studies women as a separate group rather than
comparatively, that is, in relation to men'. This is an absurdity, and
an impossibility (and indeed Alford does make statements which
are comparative, if unsystematic, throughout the book). But her
avoidance of systematic comparison undermines her ability to
explain the sexual division of labour. She attributes it to the fact
that the main economic activities were those which in Britain were
thought of as male. This seems inadequate. The sexual division of
labour in Britain itself at this time was undergoing considerable
change, and women had long been important in agriculture. In any
case, we know from examples such as the two world wars this
century that traditional notions of what constitute male and female
jobs can be radically disturbed when there is a shortage of labour. So
the exclusion of women from a wide range of occupations deserves
further analysis. Perhaps the continuing demand for and shortage of
domestic servants is explanation enough; a conclusion which would
make it all the more important that a detailed examination of this
industry be undertaken.

   Alford presents us with a paradox—that domestic servants were
in great demand, yet female convict domestic servants were often
sent back to the government by private employers. Alford suggests
that the cheapness and availability of convict servants were offset
by the fact that the women were regarded as immoral and
unmanageable. Her explanation here—that judgments about sexual
immorality overrode economic considerations—strikes me as un-
convincing. It seems at least possible that other considerations
operated. Convict women who were not sent out to service were
employed at the Parramatta Female Factory. Their labour there,
especially in laundry work and textile manufacture, was valuable,
and it seems likely that the governing authorities were quite happy
to keep a significant proportion of the women there.

   Perhaps though, on the other hand, employer complaints of
unmanageability had some validity. Whereas for the men bad
behaviour brought physical punishment and perhaps relocation to
an even more remote colonial settlement, for the women it meant
being sent to the Female Factory. Who wouldn't be unmanageable
when the choice lay between trying to survive on low or nonexistent wages amongst a sex-starved male population with no or
few female companions on a remote farm or sheep station, and
working together with women of one's own class and kind? And for
those whose preferred form of eventual escape was marriage, then
they were as likely or, probably, more likely to find a marriage
partner while at the town-based Factory as on a remote sheep farm.

So no wonder convict women deliberately committed offences in order to be sent to the Factory.

Fourth, Alford's analysis suffers from her indecision over the importance of class differences for her analysis of, as she puts it, women as a group. She does stress that women of different classes had differing employment options, but this is overshadowed by her emphasis on the fact that marriage was seen as the ideal occupation for all of them. And she gives us no sense of the class structure of colonial society. This can be seen from the way she organises women for discussion into the categories of convicts, assisted immigrants, and unassisted immigrants. These are not classes as such at all, and we need an account of how a working class, a professional middle class, a self-employed class, and an employing class developed. While it is true that the working class was supplied mainly by convicts, ex-convicts, and assisted immigrants, while other social classes were supplied mainly by unassisted immigrants (those who could afford to pay their own way), to analyse women according to their method of arrival in the colonies is limited and misleading. In particular it leads to a neglect of the women born in Australia, a significant proportion of white women by 1850. Even within the framework Alford uses, her analysis is inadequate, for the origins of these various categories of incoming women are not examined in detail. We know from other sources that the vast majority of the convict and assisted immigrant women had been domestic servants in Britain. This would seem important for any analysis of the uses to which their labour was put in the colonies.

Fifth, Alford is unclear about the pressures leading towards and against marriage. Her discussion of ideology on this matter is concerned largely with the upper-class official view. She tends to slide from her analysis of the views of upper-class males to talking of colonial ideology in general. We get little idea of *working-class* ideas about women's proper role, and not a great deal on working-class sexual mores. She does indicate that for the British working class in the early nineteenth century, and its offshoots in the Australian colonies, legal marriage was not a preferred institution until the 1850s, and that cohabitation and de facto relationships were common. If this is so, then one could expect a much more detailed examination of working-class sexual mores and family life than we get in this book.

Even upper-class sexual mores are not well dealt with. We are told that the authorities advocated marriage as a source of social stability. But we don't find out if they consequently set out—either in Britain or the colonies—to increase the female percentage of the convict intake and, indeed, we don't find out whether convict women were more or less likely than men to be given a transportation sentence. Given that 15 per cent of the convicts were women, and that the female percentage of all prisoners is usually much lower than this, it seems likely that women were transported more readily than men. Nor do we learn much about the conflicts between the state authorities and the employers on the question of marriage and female transportation. We are told employers preferred single male labour, without encumbrances (that is, wives and children) as it could be cheaper. But we don't find out if this preference brought them into conflict with the British and colonial authorities, who had more general questions of social order to consider.

Lastly, Alford confuses us on the issue of the relation between marriage and paid work for working-class women. In general, she presents marriage as the end of wage labour for women, unless they were convicts. She portrays marriage as the means whereby women of all classes are cut off from participation in other, non-domestic activities. But towards the end of the book, it becomes clear that this is not in fact the case. Not only did married rural women, from the poorest to all but the most wealthy, participate substantially in farming work, but there was also the practice of paying a family wage for married couples who were both domestic servants, agricultural labourers or teachers. This wage was more than a man's wage, but less than a male plus female wage taken together. Further examination would, I strongly suspect, reveal that married working-class women did not cease all wage labour, but continued a variety of tasks for income, at least on a casual basis.

All these problems stem from one basic source: the decision to write a history of white colonial women as a separate group. Clearly they were not a separate group, for they were economically, sexually, socially, culturally and politically interconnected with white colonial men. The conceptualisation of these women as a separate group continually leads Alford into methodological difficulties. This is a problem facing a great deal of Australian feminist history. Such a conceptual starting point leads one inexorably on to stress what these women had in common at the expense of a sustained analysis of what divided them, or what particular classes of women had in common with the male members of their class. Further, the search for that element common to all women seems to lead inevitably towards an emphasis on sexual and gender ideology. Alford's book treats this ideology much as many other feminist histories have done: as an unproblematic, uncontested one which dictates for all women a confined social and economic role. This ideology seems to float in the air, with its origins, bases and props, its interconnections and refractions, unclear.

So the disappointing feature of Alford's book is that it does not take us beyond the schema for analysis propounded by Anne Summers in her 1975 book *Damned Whores and God's Police*. Summers' book was an advance at the time, since it brought to our attention the importance of sexist ideology in the foundations of colonial society. It called a halt to male historians' absurd moralising about convict women—which was taken straight from the upper-class male condemnation of the early colonial period—and argued instead that convict women, far from being immoral and depraved, were the victims, in modern parlance, of sexual exploitation and harassment.

But now we can see some serious limitations in Summers' work. As the historian Kay Daniels has pointed out, Summers failed to investigate what convict women, and convict men, thought about sexual morality and the proper social role for women and men.[4] Summers failed, that is, to explain ideological and class conflict in the sexual arena. We are entitled to expect that Alford would have taken the argument further, especially in view of her background as an economic historian. But she does not. Like Summers she sees the ideals of marriage and family as something imposed by the state for the sake of social stability, and subsequently endorsed and promoted by upper- and middle-class women and men alike. Surely this is much too simple. Such an analysis does not take into account working-class aspirations and ideals. For working-class people, especially women, the battle for a stable and secure family life may have been seen as positive. Not just in the sense of a protection from sexually predatory males, but in the sense that these women may have wanted to care for their children themselves, and to re-establish extensive kinship ties of the kind they once knew. They may have regarded childcaring and domestic labour not as 'cutting them off from society', but as securing them a place in it. In the world *they* inhabited, such a life may have seemed an attractive option.

It is time to recast our questions about these matters. We could take as our focus the tasks of childcaring and domestic labour and ask how in early colonial society these tasks were economically supported in each social class. How, that is, was the production and reproduction of each social class made possible? We might ask how the people in each social class conducted their lives within the constraints imposed in that particular kind of society? How did expectations and daily reality conflict?

We can be certain that public interest in this early colonial period will increase. It is important that new ways of understanding the class, gender and race relations of the period be generated. It's important that the understanding of the lives of white working-class women in this period go beyond the conflicting stereotypes of 'damned whores' and 'helpless victims'. The whole field is ripe for a radical revision.

We can begin drawing up a balance sheet on the effects of feminist theory on the writing of Australian history. On the positive side we must count the bringing into view of people and activities which earlier historians forgot. Feminism has linked with the moves towards social history in opening up new areas for analysis: family life, work experiences, gender ideologies, and so on. It has made a more sympathetic treatment of outcasts such as convict women possible. Alford's additional detail on these matters does contribute to this process.

But on the negative side, feminist history like Alford's has a weak theoretical basis. It has not yet come to terms with how to explain the sexual division of labour, the economics of domestic labour, the production of and the conflict within the ideologies of sex and gender. In particular, it has not yet learnt how to make working-class people of the past, women and men, speak to us. What we have is on the one hand an assertion of oppression without explanation and, on the other, a casting of women as objects and victims rather than as historical subjects. When we do finally learn more about who *they* were, we will understand a little better who *we* are.

19

Post-colonialism, ethnic identity, and gender

I had criticised Alford, as I had Anne Summers ten years earlier, for the lack of attention to Aboriginal women in her history. There was little crossover, even by the mid-1980s, between women's, ethnic/migration, and Aboriginal history. Anthropologists such as Diane Bell had focused on Aboriginal women, but it was rare for histories of Aboriginal–European relations to take on board an interest in gender.[1] There were some exceptions. One was the work of Diane Barwick, an anthropologist turned historian, which included important accounts of the meaning of mission life in the late nineteenth and twentieth centuries for Aboriginal women in particular. Another exception was Lyndall Ryan's The Aboriginal Tasmanians, *which constructed a picture of the past where Aboriginal women were not merely the passive victims of sealers and whalers but rather people who actively negotiated with them. By and large, though, 'Aboriginal' and 'women's' history rarely overlapped.*

There was a major difference in the two kinds of history. Whereas women's history was predominantly written by women (though there were some important male contributors to the field), the history of Aboriginal–European relations was largely written by non-Aboriginal people. This situation reflected the different degrees of access to tertiary education held by white women and Aboriginal people, as well as their very different proportions of the Australian population. Yet this situation was changing by the mid-1980s, with written histories authored by Aboriginal people emerging.[3] An important aspect of this process was the development of a more self-conscious Aboriginal oral history, transcribed into print.

Further, by the mid-1980s similar questions were being asked in

145

both kinds of historical work, as historians became aware that they had been writing in a way which denied agency to the Aboriginal people and/or white women they had been writing about. They had been more interested in the processes of exploitation than in the ways its victims handled and resisted it. Recent historical work has attempted to come to terms with this problem in a variety of ways. There has been greater attention to the significance of who researches and writes history; there have also been attempts to discover and reconstruct the subjectivity of individuals and groups who have not left their own accounts, their own version of events.

For myself, I had not been able to combine my work in Aboriginal history and the history of racism generally in Australia, with my work in Australian women's history. I had been involved in a similar intellectual endeavour in each case, of arguing for the importance of class analysis, whether one looked at colonial confrontation, ethnicity, or gender. I'd made the case in relation to racism in my PhD, and summarised it in an essay entitled 'Racism and Class in Nineteenth-Century Australia' in 1984.[4] I'd made it in relation to gender in the essays reprinted in this book. Yet I had not been able to combine all three terms—race, class, and gender—in my historical work. It was in an attempt to do this that I began in 1986 a project on the sexual dimension of Aboriginal–European relations on the boundaries of European settlement.

The question of class was, I thought, important not only for theoretical but for political reasons. In 1986 I gave a paper to a conference on Culture/Media/Politics *in Sydney. My emphasis was less on theoretical problems and more on the political consequences of a social theory which* replaced *'class' with concepts such as 'ethnicity', 'national identity' and 'gender', rather than using a class analysis to illuminate the workings of each. Some people at the conference really liked the paper, but I had the impression that it was too far away from where most people were at to spark off much real debate. A section of the paper is reprinted below.*

1986

Australia is not only an industrial capitalist society; it is also a post-colonial society. In this society, the Left has fragmented into a series of movements based on particular forms of oppression. The search in the Australian Left for a particularity of oppression, for forms of oppression other than class, derives in its current form at least from the emergence of the New Left in the 1960s. Made up largely of students and young members of the professionally trained, the New Left put forward a style of politics which concentrated very little on the bread-and-butter issues that had so long occupied the labour movement, and very much on the quality of life issues concerning lifestyle, sexuality, participatory forms of politics, and so on. It argued that the working class in the advanced capitalist nations had been coopted and bought off, through the trade union movement and various other means: consumerism; commodity fetishism; the mass media and mass culture; ideological subservience to racism and sexism. The only true sources of opposition and radicalism would henceforth come from other groups. In the early stages the new source of radicalism was to be the student movement; later it was to be groups defined by virtue of a specific oppression— women, Aborigines, migrants, gays.

From this kind of political theory and inspiration came a lively period in radical politics. Aboriginal movements put their case in the public arena, for example through the Tent Embassy of 1972. The women's movement became infinitely larger, stronger, and more aggressive, than it had previously been. The gay movement became a serious political reality for the first time. The renewed emphasis on sources of division and social structuration other than class was liberating, allowing for a more complex and illuminating understanding of the way our society works. I participated in the academic and intellectual side of these developments with energy in the early 1970s, and it was exciting.

But subsequently we have had to face problems with this kind of political analysis. Each attempt to claim representativeness for a particular oppressed group finds that that group must be further broken down into even more specialised forms of oppression. The women's movement cannot speak equally for black and white women. The Aboriginal movement must come to terms with differences between Aboriginal men and Aboriginal women. And so on.

This process is most clearly seen in the women's movement. Very often the most biting critiques of feminism have come from politically active Aboriginal and non-British migrant women, who resent the men of their groups being classed as 'the enemy' while well-off Anglo-Australian women class themselves as 'oppressed'. They argue eloquently for a recognition by Anglo-Australian feminists of the importance of racism. These non-Anglo-Australian women do not reject the notion of sexism, but refuse to place it at the centre of their political strategy. As Pat O'Shane has put it, 'whereas for the majority of women involved in the women's movement, sexism is what the grand fight is all about, for Aboriginal women ... it becomes very clear that our major fight is against racism'.[5] Or, as Maureen Watson put it, 'If I am asked what I am, first of all, my answer would be: first I am black—secondly a woman. Because that is the way we are seen in this society. So that is the way I categorise my identity. But there is no way sexism can be condoned in the black struggle—no way at all'.[6]

In particular, non-Anglo women often resent the feminist critique of the family, which, based as it is on the picture of the Anglo-Australian small tight obsessive nuclear unit, bears little relation to their own experience of the family and kinship networks as profoundly important forms of economic and emotional survival. For women who have experienced the forced break-up of families, as in Aboriginal women having their children taken away from them by white authorities for the greater part of this century, the family becomes a site of resistance rather than of oppression.

A similar point has also been made by ethnic minority women elsewhere, notably in Britain and the United States. As in Australia, such women have resented white feminist assumptions that their own targets—the family, discrimination in employment, anti-abortion laws—are the targets of women everywhere. As Floya Anthias and Nira Yuval-Davis put it in a 1983 article entitled 'Contextualising feminism—gender, ethnic and class divisions', western feminist struggles are concerned with 'culturally and historically specific issues relevant mainly to middle-class white women'. They argue that all three forms of social division—class, gender, ethnicity—are 'framed in relation to each other'. None is less 'real' than the other two, none is the most important.[7]

There has, however, been a shift from asserting the importance of these particular forms to asserting that they undermine the possibility of a common radical project or debate. It is argued that nothing of value can be said about the position or policies of a particular group of people other than by members of that group. Thus only women can say anything of value about the position or the strategy of the women's movement, only Aborigines likewise, ditto non-English-speaking migrants. White men cannot speak about white women, white women about black women, and so on. And so we are all reduced to categories which supposedly define us and what we think and feel—we become white heterosexual women, or black homosexual men, or whatever. Paradoxically the refusal of the right to speak for some confers that right on all members of a named group so that the representativeness of a group member's experience or opinion is unable to be questioned by a non-member.

Analysis is in this way confined to a smaller and smaller canvas. Attempts to understand experience across gender and ethnic lines become rarer, and when they exist are open to condemnation and ridicule. So we all become highly specific entities whose right to speak at all is severely limited, whose task of understanding or of forming political alliances is negligible and narrow. Men who attempt to come to terms with feminism, for example, are silenced, sent away, very often vilified. Many of the movements lose active allies, and those who support their cause can only do so silently, often having little or no avenue for demonstrating that support politically or culturally. Our problem now is how to regain a belief in the possibility and effectiveness of collective action across gender and racial boundaries, without losing that understanding of specific cultural situations that we have so painfully begun to acquire.

Conclusion

'We go back. We ask what happened then.' Sometimes we can get a sense of direction by glancing back and then forward; we can then choose where to go next. This book has been an exercise in looking back, in order to work out where forward actually is.

One conclusion I came to, as I got out the old women's liberation newspapers and feminist journals and magazines, and read over all my own material from beginning to end, was how autobiographical intellectual work really is, and how true it is that political movements give rise to particular kinds of theoretical exploration. The women's liberation movement provides just one example. While the reader will have found that the arguments in the later chapters of this book contradict and oppose quite strongly the earlier ones, I nevertheless value the intellectual work that we did in the early seventies. We were breaking free from the commonsense knowledge of the 1960s, and we were setting ourselves new theoretical tasks and worked hard at trying to carry them out.

What are our theoretical tasks now? The problem, of course, is that many of us are trying to approach this problem theoretically. That is, we are too often not being inspired to undertake particular kinds of theoretical work as a result of involvement in a political or social movement.

There are some key exceptions, however. I'll conclude just by mentioning those with which I am most involved.

One is the continuing effects of a colonial past. In Australia, in view of the validity of Aboriginal demands for a different relation with non-Aboriginal society (land rights, better economic conditions, education, health services, and so on), it seems important to continue investigations, with non-Aboriginal people working in dialogue with Aboriginal investigators, into the history of relations between Aborigines and others in Australia, and especially of the gender/sexual dimension of those relations.

The importance of women as workers, and the continuing effects of a sexual division of labour both within the workforce itself and in

150

relation to the tasks of domestic labour and childcaring, also suggest that it is important to study the major changes historically in the relationship between women, work, and family. After years of engagement with this issue, it still strikes me as fundamentally important—theoretically, socially, and politically.

A third is to develop an understanding of how and why it is that cultural life—as expressed through film, theatre, television, music, dance, art, architecture, and writing, to name just a few—is so profoundly divided by class, and gender. I've not dealt with this in this book, though I have been engaged in an attempt to understand television, in terms both of its origins and its cultural products, for some years.[1] Given the importance of culture, in this sense, in constituting social and political life, then cultural analysis must stay high on any agenda.

And finally, there is for me a need to rethink the role of the academic historian in relation to social life and social change. This includes a greater recognition than hitherto that versions of history are produced not only in the academy, and even there not only for the academy, but in many other contexts as well—in film and television, in museums and historic sites, in local-history societies, in genealogy, in official and unofficial and anti-official commemorations of historic events. The changing locus of the practice of 'history' will have profound effects on the ways in which it is researched, presented, and understood.[2]

This seems to be enough to be going on with . . .

Notes

1 Women's liberation and the writing of history

1 See, for example, Evelyn Reed *Problems of Women's Liberation* New York 1969, p. 9.
2 R. Gollan *Radical and Working Class Politics: A Study of Eastern Australia 1850–1910* Melbourne 1967, pp. 177–80; Manning Clark *Select Documents in Australian History 1851–1900* Sydney 1968, pp. 390–99.
3 One possible exception to this is Russel Ward, in *The Australian Legend* Melbourne 1966, pp. 94–101.

4 Men and childcare

1 John and Vivian Newson *Patterns of Infant Care in an Urban Community* Harmondsworth 1966.
2 Jill Johnston *Lesbian Nation* New York 1971.

6 The Emergence of a feminist labour history

1 See Merle Thornton 'Women's Labour', in Ann Curthoys, Susan Eade and Peter Spearritt (eds) *Women at Work* Canberra 1975.
2 Anne Summers 'Bibliography: Women in Australia: Part One' *Refractory Girl* 1, 1972–73.
3 Eve Pownall *Mary of Maranoa: A memorial to the pioneer women of Australia 1788–1938* Sydney 1938; Frances Fraser and Nettie Palmer (eds) *Centenary Gift Book* Melbourne 1934; Louise Brown et al. (eds) *A Book of South Australia: Women in the First Hundred Years* Adelaide 1936; Margaret Kiddle *Caroline Chisholm* Melbourne 1950; Dianne Scott 'Womanhood suffrage: the movement in Australia' *Journal of the Royal Australian Historical Society* 53, 4, Dec. 1967, pp. 299–322.
4 *Hecate* 1, 2, July 1975, p. 40.
5 For a more detailed account, see Penny Ryan and Tim Rowse 'Women, Arbitration, and the Family' in Curthoys et al (eds) *Women at Work.*
6 See ibid. and Constance Larmour 'Women's wages and the W.E.B.' in *Women at Work,* for more detailed discussions of the Women's Employment Board.

7 For a clear statistical analysis of the situation in Sydney see Peter Spearritt 'Women in Sydney Factories, c. 1920–1950' in *Women at Work*.

8 *Hecate* 1, 2, July 1975, pp. 25–33.

9 Thornton's essay, referred to above, is a useful guide to this literature. See also Pat Vort Ronald 'Women and Class' and Mia Campioni et al. 'Opening the Floodgates: Domestic Labour and Capitalist Production' *Refractory Girl* 7, 1974.

8 Women—a 'Reserve Army of Labour'?

1 Bettina Cass, The Australian Woman's Home is her Factory (or Cottage Industry), or, Woman's Place in the Class Structure, paper delivered at SAANZ conference La Trobe University, Melbourne 1976. See also Cass 'Women's Place in the Class Structure' in E.L. Wheelwright and K. D. Buckley (eds) *Essays in the Political Economy of Australian Capitalism* vol. 3, Sydney 1978; Summers *Damned Whores* pp. 445, 466; Ryan and Rowse, 'Women, Arbitration and the Family' p. 17.

2 Kate Millett *Sexual Politics* London 1971, p. 40.

3 Ruth Milkman suggests in 'Women's Work and the Economic Crisis: Some Lessons from the Great Depression' *The Review of Radical Political Economy* 8, 1, 1976 that the reserve army thesis has risen to the level of a dogma in both the women's movement and the Left in the USA. She quotes particularly from Margaret Benston 'The Politics of Women's Liberation' *Monthly Review* 21, 1969. She also suggests, erroneously in my view, that Juliet Mitchell employs the concept in *Woman's Estate* New York 1971.

4 For Australia see particularly the work of Margaret Power: 'The Wages of Sex' *Australian Quarterly* 48, 1, March 1974; 'The Making of a Woman's Occupation' *Hecate* 1, 2, July 1975; 'Women's Work is Never Done By Men—A socioeconomic model of sex typing in occupations' *Journal of Industrial Relations* 17, 3, Sept. 1975; 'Women in the Australian Labour Market' in E. L. Wheelwright and Frank Stilwell (eds) *Readings in Political Economy* vol. 2, Sydney 1976; 'Cast Off Jobs: Women, Migrants, Blacks may apply' *Refractory Girl* 11, 1976.

5 Summers *Damned Whores* pp. 396–413.

6 Andree Wright 'The Women's Weekly: Depression and the War Years—Romance and Reality' *Refractory Girl* 3, 1973.

9 Explaining the sexual division of labour

1 Norma Grieve and Patricia Grimshaw *Australian Women: Feminist Perspectives* Melbourne 1981.

10 Radical feminism

1 Meaghan Morris 'A–mazing Grace: Notes on Mary Daly's Poetics' *Intervention* 16, 1982.

12   Politics and sisterhood

1 Kate Millett *Sexual Politics* New York 1970, p. 36.
2 Jenny Somerville 'Women: A Reserve Army of Labour?' *m/f* 7, 1982, p.57.
3 Heidi Hartmann 'The Unhappy Marriage of Marxism and Feminism: Towards a More Progressive Union' *Capital and Class* 8, 1979.

13   A short history of feminism: 1970–1984

1 Dorothy Broom *Unfinished Business: Women and Social Justice in Australia* Sydney 1984.
2 Juliet Mitchell *Woman's Estate* Harmondsworth 1971.
3 Margaret Benston 'The Political Economy of Women's Liberation' *Monthly Review* 21, 4, 1969 pp. 13–27.
4 Peggy Morton 'A woman's work is never done, or: The production, maintenance, and reproduction of labour power' *Leviathan* May 1970, reprinted in Ellen Malos (ed.) *The Politics of Housework* London 1980.
5 Rayna Rapp Reiter 'The Search for Origins: Unravelling the Threads of Gender Hierarchy' *Critique of Anthropology* 3, 9 & 10, 1977, p.7.
6 For a later critique of this approach, see Moira Gatens 'A critique of the sex/gender distinction' in Judith Allen and Paul Patton (eds) *Beyond Marxism: Interventions after Marx* Sydney 1983.
7 Shulamith Firestone *The Dialectic of Sex* New York 1970.
8 Kate Millett *Sexual Politics* New York 1970, pp. 25–33.
9 ibid. p.25.
10 Rosemary Pringle and Ann Game 'Labor in power: the feminist response' *Arena* 41, 1976, pp. 71–78.
11 See for example the article by Joyce Stevens in *Australian Left Review* 84, 1983.
12 Selma James and M. Dalla Costa 'Women and the subversion of the community' in *Radical America* 6, 1, pp. 67–102.
13 Mia Campioni et al. 'Opening the Floodgates: Domestic Labour and Capitalist Production' *Refractory Girl* 7, 1974, pp. 10–14.
14 Theresa Brennan 'Women and Work' *Journal of Australian Political Economy* 1, 1977, pp. 34–52.
15 See J. Gardiner, S. Himmelweit and M. Mackintosh 'Women's Domestic Labour' *Bulletin of the Conference of Socialist Economists* 4, 3, 1975, pp. 1–11.
16 Veronica Beechey 'Some Notes on Female Wage Labour in Capitalist Production' *Capital and Class* 3, 1977, pp. 45–66.
17 Harry Braverman *Labor and Monopoly Capital* New York 1974.
18 See especially Women's Employment Rights Campaign *Women and Unemployment* Chippendale 1979; special issue of *Refractory Girl* 18/19, 1980; Ann Game and Rosemary Pringle *Gender at Work* Sydney 1983.
19 Kay Hargreaves *Women at Work* Ringwood 1982.
20 Susan Brownmiller *Against Our Will: Men, Women and Rape* Harmondsworth 1975; Mary Daly *Gyn/Ecology: The Meta-Ethics of Radical Feminism* London 1978.

21 Daly *Gyn/Ecology* p. 28.
22 Sheila Rowbotham *Women's Consciousness, Man's World* Harmonds-worth 1973.
23 Judith Allen 'Marxism and the Man Question: Some implications of the patriarchy debate' in Judith Allen and Paul Patton (eds) *Beyond Marxism? Interventions after Marx* Sydney 1983.
24 Ann Game and Rosemary Pringle *Gender at Work* Sydney 1983.
25 Gayle Rubin, 'The Traffic in Women: Notes on the Political Economy of Sex' in R. Reiter (ed.) *Toward an Anthropology of Women* New York 1975.
26 Jill Julius Matthews *Good and Mad Women: The Historical Construction of Femininity in Twentieth-Century Australia* Sydney 1984, pp. 13–14.

14 Women and class

1 Michele Barrett *Women's Oppression Today* London 1980.

15 The family and feminism

1 Kate Millett *Sexual Politics* p. 33.
2 Lorraine Mortimer 'Feminism and Motherhood' *Arena* 73, 1985.

16 Theories of the sexual division of labour

1 For a discussion of problems in conceptualisation and measurement, see Irene Bruegel 'Women's Employment, Legislation, and the Labour Market' in Jane Lewis (ed.) *Women's Welfare/Women's Rights* London 1983, pp. 130–69; Sandra Eccles 'Overview of women's employment in Australia' in Mavis Hoy (ed.) *Women in the Labour Force: The Proceedings of a Conference* Canberra 1985, pp. 1–23; D. E. Lewis 'The Measurement of the Occupational and Industrial Segregation of Women' *Journal of Industrial Relations* 24, Sept. 1982, pp. 406–23; and C. Hakim 'Job Segregation: Trends in the 1970s' *Employment Gazette* 89, 12, Dec. 1981, pp. 521–33.
2 Ruth Milkman 'Redefining "women's work": the Sexual Division of Labour in the Auto Industry during World War II' *Feminist Studies* 8, 2, Summer 1982, p. 366.
3 OECD Working Party on the Role of Women in the Economy, 'Occupational Segregation by Sex', quoted in Margaret Power, C. Wallace, S. Outhwaite and S. Rosewarne *Women, Work and Labour Market Programs* (commissioned by the Committee of Inquiry into Labour Market Programs) Sydney 1985.
4. Cynthia B. Lloyd and Beth T. Niemi *The Economics of Sex Differentials* New York 1979.
5 See note 3.
6 D. E. Lewis 'Measurement of Occupational and Industrial Segregation of Women' p. 418.
7 Ann Oakley *Sex, Gender and Society* London 1972.
8 Veronica Beechey 'The Sexual Division of Labour and the Labour Process: a Critical Assessment of Braverman' in Stephen Wood (ed.) *The Degradation of Work* London 1983, pp. 54–73.

9   See William Lazonick 'The Subjection of Labour to Capital: the Rise
    of the Capitalist System *Review of Radical Political Economics* 10, 1,
    Spring 1978, pp. 1–52, and Ivy Pinchbeck *Women Workers and the
    Industrial Revolution 1750–1850* London 1981, first publ. 1930.
10 Margaret Power 'The Making of a Woman's Occupation' *Hecate* 1, 2,
    July 1975, pp. 25–34.
11 Eileen Byrne 'Women's Vocational Choices and Career Paths: Princi-
    pal Issues' in Hoy *Women in the Labour Force.* See also P. D. Earley
    'Girls, School and Work: Technological Change and Female Entry
    into the Non-traditional Work Areas' *Australian Journal of Education*
    25, 3, 1981, pp. 269–86.
12 Byrne 'Women's Vocational Choices' p. 147.
13 J. Mincer 'Labor Force Participation of Married Women: a Study of
    Labour Supply' in *Aspects of Labor Economics: A Report of the
    National Bureau of Economic Research* Princeton, NJ. 1962, pp.
    62–105; J. Mincer and Solomon Polachek 'Family Investments in
    Human Capital: Earnings of Women' *Journal of Political Economy* 82,
    2, pt 2, March–April 1974, pp. 76–108; S. Polachek 'Discontinuous
    Labor Force Participation and its Effect on Women's Market Ear-
    nings' in C. Lloyd (ed.) *Sex, Discrimination, and the Division of
    Labour* New York 1975.
14 P. Doeringer and M. Piore *Internal Labour Markets and Manpower
    Analysis* Lexington, Mass. 1971.
15 For useful summaries of this position see Alice H. Amsden *The
    Economics of Women and Work* New York 1979, and Irene Bruegel
    'Women's Employment Legislation and the Labour Market' in Jane
    Lewis (ed.) *Women's Welfare/Womens' Rights.*
16 Richard Edwards *Contested Terrain: The Transformation of the
    Workplace in the Twentieth Century* New York 1979.
17 Richard Kreckel 'Unequal Opportunity Structure and Labor Market
    Segmentation' *Sociology* 14, 5, Nov. 1980, pp. 524–50.
18 Richard C. Edwards, Michael Reich and David Gordon (eds) *Labor
    Market Segmentation* Lexington, Mass. 1975.
19 ibid. p. 19.
20 R. D. Barron and G.M. Norris 'Sexual Divisions and the Dual Labour
    Market' in Diana Leonard Barker and Sheila Allen (eds) *Dependence
    and Exploitation in Work and Marriage* London 1976, pp. 47–69.
    Francine D. Blau and Caro L. Jusenius 'Economists' Approaches to
    Sex Segregation in the Labor Market: an Appraisal' in Martha Blaxall
    and Barbara Reagan (eds) *Women and the Workplace* Chicago 1975.
21 Desley Deacon 'The Employment of Women in the Commonwealth
    Public Service: the Creation and Reproduction of a Dual Labour
    Market *Australian Journal of Public Administration* XLI, 3, September
    1982, pp. 232–50; and 'State Formation, the New Middle Class and
    the Dual Labour Market: Women Clerks in an Australian Bureaucracy
    1880–1930' in Gwen Moore and Glenna Spitze (eds) *Women and
    Politics: Activism, Attitudes and Office Holdings* 2 in Research in
    Politics and Society, JAI Press 1985.
22 Jock Collins 'A Divided Working Class' *Intervention* 8, 1977, pp.
    64–78, and Jock Collins 'Fragmentation of the Working Class' in E. L.

Wheelwright and K. D. Buckley (eds) *Essays in the Political Economy of Australian Capitalism* vol. I, Sydney 1978.

23 Edmund S. Phelps 'The Statistical Theory of Racism and Sexism' *American Economic Review* 62, 4, Sept. 1972, pp. 659–61. See also Amsden for a useful summary of this argument.

24 Bruce Chapman 'Sex and Location Differences in Wages in the Australian Public Service' *Discussion Paper* no. 98, Centre for Economic Policy Research, ANU, July 1984.

25 D. E. Lewis 'Comparative Quit Rates of Men and Women' *Journal of Industrial Relations* 21, Sept. 1979, pp. 331—50.

26 Jane Humphries 'The Working Class Family, Women's Liberation and Class Struggle: the Case of Nineteenth Century British History' *Review of Radical Political Economics* 9, 3, Autumn 1977, pp. 25–41.

27 Theresa Brennan 'Women and Work' *Journal of Australian Political Economy* 1, Oct. 1977, pp. 34–52.

28 Heidi Hartmann 'Capitalism, Patriarchy and Job Segregation by Sex' in Blaxall and Reagan *Women in the Workplace*.

29 Ruth Milkman 'Organising the Sexual Division of Labour: Historical Perspectives on Women's Work and the American Labor Movement' *Socialist Review* 10, 49, Jan.–Feb. 1980, pp. 95–150.

30 Michelle Barrett and Mary McIntosh 'The Family Wage: Some Problems for Socialists and Feminists' *Capital and Class* 11, 1980, pp. 51–73.

31 Claire Williams *Open Cut: The Working Class in an Australian Mining Town* Sydney 1981.

32 Johanna Brenner and Maria Ramas 'Rethinking Women's Oppression' *New Left Review* 144, March/April 1984, pp. 33–71.

33 Ann Curthoys 'The Sexual Division of Labour Under Capitalism' in Norma Grieve and Patricia Grimshaw (eds), *Australian Women: Feminist Perspectives* Melbourne 1981.

34 Edna Ryan and Anne Conlon *Gentle Invaders: Australian Women at Work, 1788–1974* Melbourne 1975.

35 Laura Bennett 'Legal Intervention and the Female Workforce: the Conciliation and Arbitration Court 1907–21' *International Journal of the Sociology of Law* 12, 1, Feb. 1984, pp. 23–36.

36 Harry Braverman *Labor and Monopoly Capital: the Degradation of Work in the Twentieth Century* New York 1974; Anne Phillips and Barbara Taylor 'Sex and Skill: Notes towards a Feminist Economics' *Feminist Review* 6, 1980, pp. 79–88.

37 Cynthia Cockburn *Brothers: Male Dominance and Technological Change* London 1983.

38 Jill Rubery 'Structured Labour Markets, Workers Organisation and Low Pay' in Amsden (ed.) *The Economics of Women and Work* pp. 242–70. See also Laura Bennett 'The Construction of Skill: Craft Unions, Women Workers and the Conciliation and Arbitration System' *Law in Context* 2, 1984, pp. 188–232.

39 Carol O'Donnell *The Basis of the Bargain* Sydney 1984. See also Jack Barbalet 'Class Theory and Earnings Inequality' *Australian and New Zealand Journal of Sociology* 21, 3, November 1985.

40 Laura Bennett 'The Construction of Skill'.

41   Carol O'Donnell *The Basis of the Bargain* p. 19.
42   Ann Game and Rosemary Pringle *Gender at Work,* Sydney, 1983.

17   The return of biology

1   Hester Eisenstein *Contemporary Feminist Thought* London and Sydney 1984.
2   In Allen and Patton *Beyond Marxism?* pp. 143–62.
3   Bob Connell 'Theorising Gender' in Norma Grieve and Ailsa Burns *Australian Women: New Feminist Perspectives* Melbourne 1986, pp. 354, 356.
4   Janet Sayers *Biological Politics* London 1982, p. 3
5   Penelope Brown and L. Jordanova 'Oppressive dichotomies: the nature/culture debate' in Elizabeth Whitelegg et al. (eds) *The Changing Experience of Women* Oxford 1982, p. 393.
6   Talcott Parsons 'The Family' in Rose L. Coser *The Family: Its Structure and Functions* 2nd edn, New York 1974, p. 15.
7   Margaret Mead *Males and Females* Harmondsworth 1962, pp. 183–84.
8   Ernestine Friedl *Women and Men: An Anthropologists's View* New York 1975, p. 8.
9   Dorothy Dinnerstein *The Mermaid and the Minotaur: Sexual Arrangements and Human Malaise* New York 1977; Nancy Chodorow *The Reproduction of Mothering* Berkeley 1978.
10   Shulamith Firestone *The Dialectic of Sex* New York 1970, p.7.
11   Evelyne Sullerot 'The Feminine (Matter of) Fact' in E. Marks and I. Courtivron (eds) *New French Feminisms* Brighton 1981, p. 158.
12   ibid.
13   ibid.
14   Mia Campioni and Elizabeth Gross 'Love's Labours Lost: Marxism and Feminism' in Judith Allen and Paul Patton (eds) *Beyond Marxism: Interventions After Marx* Sydney 1983, p. 132.
15   Sayers *Biological Politics* p. 200.

18   Colonial women's history

1   Published by Oxford University Press
2   Marilyn Lake and Farley Kelly (eds) *Double Time: Women in Victoria 150 Years* Ringwood 1985; Patricia Crawford (ed.) *Exploring Women's Past: Essays in Social History* Carlton 1983; Patricia Grimshaw, Chris McConville and Ellen McEwen (eds) *Families in Colonial Australia* Sydney 1985; and Kerreen Reiger *The Disenchantment of the Home: Modernising the Australian Family 1880–1940* Melbourne 1985.
3   Only twice, on pages 20 and 44, does Alford mention the prostitution of Aboriginal women, and then only in passing. The only other mention of Aborigines is two references to white middle-class women's fear or dislike of them (pp. 140, 148), and a footnote (p. 92) explaining that the economic role of Aboriginal women is not dealt with owing to a paucity of sources. The sources are limited, but not as limited as Alford suggests. To the two works cited by Alford in her

footnote, F. Gale (ed.) *Women's Role in Aboriginal Society* Canberra 1974, and L. Ryan *The Aboriginal Tasmanians* St. Lucia 1981, the latter by the way yielding considerable information which Alford could have used, must be added: Henry Reynolds *The Other Side of the Frontier* Ringwood 1982; R.H.W. Reece *Aborigines and Colonists: Aborigines and Colonial Society in New South Wales in the 1830s and 1840s* Sydney 1974; Judith Wright *The Cry for the Dead* Melbourne 1981 and a number of others. Both Ryan and Reynolds, in particular, have shown that histories *can* transcend the white male bias of their sources.

4 'Women's History', in G. Osborne and W.F. Mandle (eds) *New History: Studying Australia Today* Sydney 1982.

19 Post-colonialism, ethnic identity and gender

1 Diane Bell *Daughters of the Dreaming* Melbourne 1983.

2 Diane Barwick 'And the lubras are ladies now' in Fay Gale (ed.) *Woman's Role in Aboriginal Society* Canberra 1974.

3 For a useful review of this body of work, see Lyndall Ryan's review article in *Meanjin* 1, 1986.

4 'Racism and Class in Nineteenth-Century Australia' in Andrew Markus and Merle Ricklefs (eds) *Surrender Australia? Historians and Professor Blainey* Sydney 1984.

5 Pat O'Shane 'Is there any relevance in the women's movement for Aboriginal Women?' *Refractory Girl* 12, 1976, p. 33.

6 Maureen Watson 'First I am black, secondly I am a woman' *Socialist Feminist Conference Bulletin* 1, 1987, pp. 2–3.

7 Floya Anthias and Nira Yuval-Davis 'Contextualising feminism—gender, ethnic and class divisions' *Feminist Review* 15, 1983.

Conclusion

1 'The Getting of Television: Dilemmas in ownership, control, and culture in Australia 1942–56' in Ann Curthoys and John Merritt (eds) *Better Dead than Red: Australia's First Cold War vol. 2,* Sydney 1986; with John Docker 'In Praise of "Prisoner" ' in Graeme Turner, forthcoming collection on Australian television.

2 For more discussion of this issue see my chapter 'Into History' in Ann Curthoys, Allan Martin, Tim Rowse (eds) *Australians Since 1939* Sydney 1987.

Index

160